BODY BUILDING COOKBOOK FOR WOMEN

Muscle-Building, Fat Burning Recipes to
Make You Stronger Than Ever

Paula Kennedy

Bodybuilding Cookbook for Women

Muscle-Building, Fat Burning Recipes to Make You Stronger Than Ever

Paula Kennedy

Disclaimer

The recipes and information in this book are provided for educational purposes only. Please always consult a licensed professional before making changes to your lifestyle or diet. The author and publisher shall have neither liability nor responsibility to anyone with respect to any loss or damage caused or alleged to be caused directly or indirectly by the information contained in this book. All trademarks and brands within this book are for clarifying purposes only and are owned by the owners themselves, not affiliated with this document.

Table of Contents

INTRODUCTION

T he perfect diet for bodybuilding is essential. It might be tough to follow any diet, especially if you aren't used to a healthy lifestyle. There are a lot of temptations and seductions that can take you off the road when following this type of dietary regimen. Forget about failures! Our cookbook has your salvation with all the science behind meal prep - it's an open world full of possibilities in making life much easier on yourself for achieving things like being more toned or having glowing skin by eating well-balanced meals made specifically tailored towards weightlifters and people who want to maintain their health while still enjoying delicious foods from time to time without feeling guilty.

The human body is a miraculous organism, one that can turn light energy from the sun into food in order to fuel its functions. Some people are given an extra advantage when it comes to this process; they have more muscles and stronger bones than others due to their activity level. This article will look at how these individuals can take this natural ability even further by using meal prepping for muscle building goals with all of its benefits!

There's no better way you could spend your time off work or school then focusing on what makes you happy: sculpting yourself into something beautiful through exercise and nutrition! We'll show you different ways we've found over our years working out together-whether it be eating like a normal person or getting buffed up.

CHAPTER 1: Muscle is Won or Lost in the Kitchen

Your body is only as good as the fuel you provide it with, so make sure to put in quality nutrients for your workout. Every ounce of sweat and effort goes down the drain if you don't give yourself a healthy diet plan. If want an awesome physique then increase your intake by 20%.

Eating for Muscle

To build muscle, you need to take in an excess of calories with the right nutrients. If you don't eat enough, your body won't be able to fully repair the damage caused by lifting weights and will even start losing muscle! However, it is important not to make that mistake most gym rats do: eating everything in sight from pizzas and pop-tarts which are unhealthy for long-term growth. Fortunately there are healthy foods out there that can help me grow without having any side effects like greasy food or being time consuming at all such as coming recipes I have included below.

Eating for Shred

The yearning for a diet that gratifies all the senses is what fuels this cookbook. The author doesn't want you to be bored with your food while on some fad diet, so she created these recipes specifically for gym-goers and athletes who need to eat well without sacrificing their favorite tastes of rich dishes like lasagna or macaroni cheese. Whether it's chicken parmesan pasta bake in tomato sauce served over spaghetti noodles or cheesy zucchini casserole made with ground turkey crumbles cooked up into a creamy layer perfect atop fresh green beans--this book has something special just waiting at every turn!

CHAPTER 2: THE FUNDAMENTAL PILLARS OF A MUSCLE BUILDING/FAT BURNING DIET

Before you ask, no, you don't need to be a nutritionist to design your ideal diet. What you need to know are a few basic concepts:

1. Define protein, carbohydrates, and fats, as well as their functions.

2. How much of each you'll need and where you'll get it from.

3. How many calories are needed to achieve your muscle-building or fat-burning objectives?

What is Protein

Protein is a macronutrient that provides your body with energy, muscle repair and growth, as well as being necessary for normal function of the immune system. Protein can be found in foods such as eggs, meat, fish, milk products, legumes (beans) beans and tofu. It's important to remember that some protein sources may not consist of all nine essential amino acids so it's best to eat a variety!

What Are Carbohydrates?

You may not know it, but carbohydrates are your best friend - they provide energy and keep us going. However, there is a difference between the two types of carbs: simple vs complex. Simple sugars like sugar can be quickly digested by the body for quick bursts of energy when you're hungry or in need to get things done fast; however complex ones take longer to convert into glucose which promotes steady blood-sugar levels throughout the day for good health!

The explanation that so many people are scared of carbohydrates is because everything your body doesn't use is stored as fat. Carbohydrates, on the other hand, are not the enemy; they are necessary for your success.

What are Fats?

Fats are a type of lipids that can be used to provide energy. Fats are also important for normal growth, development and function of your body's cells. A lot of fats consist on omega-three fatty acids which is an anti inflammatory agent that aids in joint pain relief and weight management.

There are four types of fat: Monounsaturated, Polyunsaturated, Saturated and Trans-fatty acids. Monounsaturated, Polyunsaturated and Saturated fats will all help you to maintain a healthy weight. These are found in avocados, almonds, olive oil and coconuts respectively. They also contain fatty acids that can help your cells function better as well as keep them strong throughout the day so they don't become damaged from inflammation or free radicals which both cause damage to our body.

Trans-Fatty acids are the only ones you can avoid. There are fats that have been lab-modified to extend their shelf life. Since the body is unsure what to do with them, they can enter your cells and cause harm. They're most commonly used in ready-to-eat meals and are used in a variety of fried foods.

How much of each do you require?

Ok, it depends on your objectives!

A GOOD PLACE TO START BUILDING MUSCLE IS:

- 1.5 grams of protein per pound of bodyweight
- 2 grams of carbohydrates per pound of bodyweight
- 0.5 grams of fat per pound of bodyweight

You should be gaining 0.5–1 pound per week. If you eat more than that, you can gain too much weight. If you aren't gaining weight, gradually raise your calorie intake by 100-200 calories per week before you meet your target weight. If you're gaining too much weight, you can cut your calories by 100 to 200 calories a week.

A GOOD PLACE TO START FOR MAINTAINING MUSCLE IS:

- 1 gram of protein per pound of bodyweight
- 1 gram of carbohydrates per pound of bodyweight
- 0.5 grams of fat per pound of bodyweight

A GOOD PLACE TO START IF YOU WANT TO LOSE WEIGHT IS:

- 2 grams of protein per pound of bodyweight
- Carbohydrates are measured in milligrams per pound of bodyweight.
- 1 gram of fat per pound of body weight

You should be losing 1–2 pounds a week. If you do any more, you risk losing the hard-won muscle. If you aren't losing weight, cut your calories by 100-200 calories a week before you meet your target weight. If you're losing too much weight, you can raise your calorie intake by 100 to 200 calories per week.

CHAPTER 3: THE TOP COMMANDMENTS OF GOOD NUTRITION

What you put into your body will determine whether or not you get good results in the gym. If you want to be effective in your muscle-building and fat-loss efforts, you must follow these guidelines.

Have protein with every meal

Protein is necessary for the body to function properly. Protein also contains amino acids which help repair cells and muscles, making them stronger than they were before. Protein can be found in red meat, eggs, chicken breast and fish respectively. Amino acids are present in plant-based protein as well such as beans or quinoa but these tend to have more carbs so it's important that you calculate your macros if this will make up a large part of your diet because too many carbohydrates could lead to weight gain.

There must be Green on the Plate

In general, vegetables are high in fiber and low in calories. They also contain vitamins to help your body stay healthy throughout the day. Some of my personal favorites include broccoli, kale and tomatoes.

Fat is not the Enemy

Let's be clear about one thing: overweight will not make you fat. It's important to get enough if you want to gain muscle and burn fat. Healthy fats are needed for the development of many hormones in the body, including testosterone, as we've established. Trans fats are the only fats you can stop.

DON'T Depend ON SUPPLEMENTS; EAT "Real" FOOD.

Supplements are intended to round out the diet rather than replace it entirely. At least 70% of your diet should be made up of 'real' foods.

MOST OF THE TIME, STAY WITH SLOW DIGESTING CARBS (EXCEPT AROUND YOUR WORKOUTS)

Slow-digesting carbohydrates have a consistent supply of energy while having a lower effect on blood sugar levels. Consuming fast-digesting carbohydrates on a regular basis has been related to an increased risk of diabetes, heart disease, and obesity. However, you can quickly replenish your depleted glycogen stocks after training to avoid catabolism and maintain your body in a "muscle-building" state. This is why, after your workout, you can eat a fast-digesting carbohydrate.

Drink Water

It's important to drink a lot of it. It will cleanse your system and hydrate your skin, muscles, and other body tissues. Water makes up 70% of your muscles, so if you're trying to gain muscle, you'll need to drink plenty of it. Get in the habit of drinking at least 1 gallon of water a day, and more if you're training for a race. Drinking more water does not help the body absorb it, contrary to common opinion. Your body, on the other hand, can learn to absorb it and help you lose weight faster.

CHAPTER 4: BREAKFAST

BRAWNY BREAKFAST BURRITO

With this Mexican-inspired burrito, you can spice up your life. It's packed with protein, healthy fats, and fiber to help you develop muscle in a lean way.

Nutrient Value

- 302 calories per serving
- 25 g protein
- Carbohydrates: 19 g
- 16g fat

Ingredients:

- 2 eggs
- 50 mL low-fat milk
- 25 g black beans
- 50 g low-fat cheese
- A handful of chopped red peppers

- 1 tsp chopped coriander
- 1 tbsp salsa
- 12 tsp cumin

Procedure

1. In a large mixing bowl, whisk together the milk, eggs, and cumin.

2. Coat a pan with cooking spray and heat on low. Fill the pan with the mixture.

3. Add the low-fat cheese, chopped red peppers, and black beans to the omelette after about 2–3 minutes.

4. Fold the omelette in half and cook through once it has been inserted (1-2 minutes).

5. Remove from the pan and toss with the salsa and coriander before serving.

BANANA AND ALMOND MUSCLE OATMEAL

This recipe is perfect if you're in a rush. It only takes about 5 minutes to prepare and contains all of the required macronutrients to make this a nutritious and filling meal.

Nutrient Value

- 523 calories per serving
- 32 g protein
- Carbohydrates: 60 g
- 15 g fat

Ingredients

- 50g rolled oat
- 200ml low-fat milk
- 1 scoop whey protein (vanilla or chocolate)

- Handful sliced almonds
- 1 tsp organic peanut butter
- 1 diced banana

Procedure:

1. Combine the oats and low-fat milk in a large microwave-safe bowl, stir, and cook for two minutes.

2. Toss the oats with the sliced banana, peanut butter, whey protein, and chopped almonds.

MASS BUILDING SWEET POTATO PANCAKES

Start your day with this delicious protein-packed pancake recipe that is fast and simple to make. It's got all the right ingredients to keep you going, as well as plenty of protein to keep your muscles happy!

Nutrient Value

- 451 calories per serving
- 38 g protein
- Carbohydrates: 74g
- 9 g fat

Ingredients

- 1 egg
- 4 egg whites
- 1 medium sweet potato
- Greek yogurt (100g fat-free)
- 40g oats

- 1 tsp cinnamon
- 1 tsp vanilla extract
- 1 tsp sugar
- A handful of diced strawberries
- A handful of blueberries

How to do it:

1. Rinse the sweet potato under cold water for a few seconds, then pierce it several times with a fork and microwave until tender (about 8 minutes).

2. Allow it to cool before removing all of the skin with a knife.

3. Blend the oats until they are a fine powder in a blender, then transfer to a cup.

4. Puree the sweet potato in a blender until creamy, then combine with the oat powder.

5. Whisk together the egg, egg whites, vanilla, cinnamon, sugar, and yogurt. This is your pancake batter at this stage.

6. Spray a pan with nonstick cooking spray and heat on low. Cook for 1-2 minutes with around a quarter of the batter in the pan.

7. Cook for another 30 seconds after flipping the pancake. Remove your delicious pancake from the oven and top with the berries. Continue with the rest of the batter in the same manner.

PROTEIN POWERED PANCAKES

If you don't like sweet potatoes, these are a perfect substitute. There's a lot of protein in this dish, and it's fast and simple to prepare.

Nutrient Value (This recipe makes around 5 pancakes.)

- 337 calories per serving
- 27 g protein
- Carbohydrates: 33 g
- 9 g fat

Ingredients

- 6 egg whites
- 40g rolled oats
- 1 tsp flaxseed oil
- 1 tsp cinnamon
- 1 tsp stevia
- Handful of small berries to serve

Procedure

1. Mix the oats with the rest of the ingredients in a blender. This is your pancake batter at this stage.

2. Coat a pan with cooking spray and heat on low.

3. Pour about one-fifth of the pancake batter into the pan and cook for one to two minutes. Cook for another 30 seconds after flipping the pancake.

4. When the pancake is finished, remove it from the pan.

5. Continue with the rest of the batter in the same manner.

6. Garnish with fresh fruit of your choosing.

SUPER SCRAMBLED TURKEY BACON EGGS ON TOAST

This delicious recipe will spice up your bland egg-based breakfasts. Since eggs contain all eight amino acids, they are a great source of complete protein.

Nutrient Value

- 299 calories per serving
- 22 g protein
- Carbohydrates: 35 g
- 8 g fat

Ingredients

- 6 egg whites
- 3 slices turkey bacon
- 2 slices Ezekiel or wholemeal bread
- 1 tsp garlic powder
- Handful of chopped onion
- Handful of chopped yellow peppers
- Handful of chopped white mushrooms
- 1 tsp olive oil
- 1 tsp dried parsley

Procedure

1. Coat a pan with cooking spray and heat it on medium/high. Cook until the chopped onions, yellow peppers, and white mushrooms are tender.

2. Cook the turkey bacon in a separate pan.

3. Scramble the egg whites with the garlic powder in the pan with the veggies and 1 tsp olive oil until the eggs are strong.

4. Remove the Ezekiel bread from the oven and toast it.

5. Add the turkey bacon to the scrambled eggs and break it up.

6. To serve, plate scrambled eggs and turkey bacon on bread with fresh parsley on top.

7. Season with salt and pepper as needed.

SCRAMBLED EGGS WITH SPINACH

Delicious, quick, and simple breakfast with a lot of protein.

Nutrient Content (Serves 2)

- 282 calories per serving
- 23 g protein
- Carbohydrates: 15 g
- 15 g fat

Ingredients

- 3 eggs
- 5 egg whites
- 1 cup baby spinach
- 50g grated low fat cheese
- A handful of chopped onion
- A handful of chopped red peppers.
- 1 tsp olive oil

Procedure

1. Coat a pan with cooking spray and heat it on medium/high.

2. Cook until the chopped onions and red peppers are tender.

3. Scramble the egg and egg whites in the pan with the vegetables and 1 tsp olive oil until the eggs are strong.

4. Top the eggs with baby spinach leaves and cheese.

5. Arrange scrambled eggs on a plate and serve.

6. Season with salt and pepper as needed.

AESTHETIC ASPARAGUS FRITTATA

This high-protein, low-carb breakfast is ideal for those who want to limit their carb intake.

Nutrient Content (Serves 3)

- 349 calories per serving
- 23 g protein
- Carbohydrates: 8 g
- 25 g fat

Ingredients

- 300 g chopped asparagus
- 12 florets only broccoli
- 8 eggs
- 100ml low-fat milk
- Handful of chopped parsley
- 1 tsp chives

- 1 tbsp olive oil
- Salt and pepper

Procedure

1. Crack the eggs into a mixing bowl, add the milk, and season with salt and pepper.

2. Steam the broccoli for 4-5 minutes in a covered skillet over medium heat. Place to the side.

3. Next, heat the oil in the same skillet. Cook the chopped asparagus, chopped parsley, and chives in a skillet over medium heat for around 2-3 minutes.

4. Pour the egg mixture into the skillet with the broccoli and evenly cover the skillet.

5. Cook for around 3-4 minutes, or until the eggs are fully set.

Place the skillet under the grill for around 2 minutes, or until golden on top (optional).

7. Arrange on a plate and eat.

TURKEY MUSCLE OMELETTE

This is the breakfast for you if you're looking for a high-protein, low-carb choice. There are 26 grams of protein and just 5 grams of carbohydrates in this shake.

Nutrient Content (Serves 2)

- 358 calories per serving
- 26 g protein
- Carbohydrates: 5 g
- 21g fat

Ingredients

- 3 eggs
- 150g chopped or minced turkey
- 1 tbsp olive oil
- 25g low-fat cheese
- 1 handful baby spinach
- 1 handful kale

Procedure

1. Crack the eggs into a mixing bowl and whisk them together.

2. In a medium-sized skillet, heat half of the oil, then add the turkey, kale, and cheese and cook for 5-6 minutes.

3. Heat the remaining olive oil in a separate pan, then add the eggs and cook for about 4 minutes.

4. Pour the turkey mixture into the pan with the eggs, cover with baby spinach, and fold the omelette in half.

5. Continue to cook for an additional 2-3 minutes.

6. Arrange on a plate and serve.

POWER PROTEIN WAFFLES

Who said waffles were bad for you? My waffle recipes are high in protein and low in calories, so you can enjoy them guilt-free!

Nutrient Content

- 314 calories per serving
- 37 g protein

- Carbohydrates: 28 g
- 5 g fat

Ingredients

- 1 spoon vanilla protein powder
- 4 egg whites
- 40g rolled oats
- 1 tsp baking powder
- 12 tsp stevia

Procedure

1. In a blender, combine all of the ingredients and blend until smooth.

2. Bake in a waffle iron with the mixture.

CHAPTER 5: CHICKEN AND POULTRY

ANABOLIC JERK CHICKEN AND BROWN RICE

This typical Caribbean dish will add a little spice to your life. To keep you rising, it's packed with protein and slow-release carbohydrates.

Nutrient Content

- 516 calories per serving
- 32 g protein
- Carbohydrates: 76g
- 33 g fat

Ingredients

- 100g thighs or breasts of chicken
- 12 tsp ground allspice
- 12 tsp black pepper
- 12 tsp nutmeg
- 12 tsp cinnamon
- 12 tsp sage
- 12 tsp dried thyme
- 1 garlic clove
- 12 tsp dried thyme
- 1 chopped onion
- 2 chopped and deseeded scotch bonnet chilies
- 12 chopped red pepper
- 60g brown rice
- 1 tsp olive oil

Procedure

1. To make the jerk paste, blend together the allspice, nutmeg, sage, cinnamon, dried thyme, garlic, red pepper, black pepper, onion, olive oil, and scotch bonnet chillies until smooth.

2. Rub the paste all over the chicken breasts and let them marinate for at least an hour.

3. Place the chicken breasts on the grill and cook for 10 to 12 minutes per hand, or until cooked through. When cooked, remove from the pan and set aside.

4. Meanwhile, fill a pot halfway with cold water and heat until it boils. When the water is boiling, add the rice and cook for 20 minutes.

5. Drain the rice and combine it with the chicken to eat.

TURKEY MEATBALL FIESTA

Healthy turkey meatballs with oats added to help you gain muscle and lose weight.

Nutrient Content (Serves 4)

- 315 calories per serving
- 35 g protein
- Carbohydrates: 23 g
- 10 g fat

Ingredients

- 500g turkey mince
- 50g rolled porridge oats
- 2 chopped spring onions
- 1 tsp ground cumin

- 1 tsp coriander
- Handful of chopped coriander
- 1 tsp olive oil
- 1 chopped red onion
- 2 chopped garlic cloves
- 1 large chopped yellow pepper
- 3 tsp chipotle chili paste

Procedure

1. Combine the mince, oats, chopped spring onions, herbs, and coriander in a mixing bowl.

2. Using your hands, shape the mince mixture into 12 tiny "meatballs."

3. Heat some olive oil in a skillet over medium heat, then add the meatballs and cook until golden.

4. Remove them from the pan and set them aside.

5. Cook until the onion, chopped pepper, and chopped garlic are tender in the pan.

6. Stir in the chilli paste, ground cumin, and chicken stock in the pan. Then return the meatballs to the pan.

7. Cook for about 10 minutes, covered, on a low/medium heat.

8. Add the tomatoes and black beans to the pan and cook for 2-3 minutes, uncovered.

9. Garnish with coriander and chopped avocado.

LAZY CHICKEN AND EGG STIR FRY

This meal is simple to prepare and provides two excellent protein sources for muscle growth and fat loss.

Nutrient Content

- 409 calories per serving
- 46 g protein
- Carbohydrates: 89g
- 20 g fat

Ingredients

- 100g chopped chicken breast
- 2 eggs
- 100g brown rice
- 2 tsp Chinese five spice
- 100g frozen mixed vegetables

Procedure

1. Fill a pot halfway with cold water and heat until it boils. When the water is boiling, add the rice and cook for 20 minutes. Remove the rice from the pot and set it aside.

2. In a medium-sized skillet, heat the chopped chicken and spices.

3. Cook for about 5 minutes in a stir-fry pan.

4. Boil or steam the frozen vegetables for 5 minutes until cooked while the chicken cooks, and beat the eggs in a separate cup.

5. Stir the rice and beaten eggs into the pan with the chicken for 3-4 minutes, or until the eggs begin to scramble.

6. Finally, add the vegetables to the pan and stir for a few minutes more.

HEALTHY TURKEY BURGERS

BURGERS WITH TURKEY THAT ARE Safe

This nutritious turkey burger will satisfy your burger cravings.

Nutrient Content (Serves 4)

- 362 calories per serving
- 38 g protein
- Carbohydrates: 39 g
- 7g fat

Ingredients

- 500g turkey mince
- 1 finely chopped onion
- 1 chopped romaine lettuce
- 4 wholemeal buns
- 2 diced tomatoes
- 1 crushed garlic clove
- 1 lemon
- 3 tbsp grated parmesan
- Chopped parsley
- 3 tbsp low-fat Greek yogurt

Procedure

1. Preheat the oven to 375°F/190°C/Gas Mark 5 (375°F/190°C/Gas Mark 5).

2. Combine the crushed garlic, 2 tablespoons parmesan, and parsley in a mixing bowl.

3. Squeeze the lemon juice over the ingredients after cutting the lemon in half. Combine all of the ingredients in a large mixing bowl.

4. Combine the ingredients in a mixing bowl with the onion and minced turkey.

5. Shape the mince mixture into four burgers with your hands, put on a baking sheet, and bake for about 20 minutes, or until the burgers are cooked through.

6. Break open the whole-wheat buns and combine the yogurt and lettuce while the burgers are cooking. Combine the burgers, yogurt-lettuce mixture, and tomatoes in the buns.

BRAWNY CHICKEN & CHORIZO JAMBALAYA

Cajun cuisine influenced this delicious muscle-building recipe. It's packed with protein and slow-release carbs to keep you burning calories and gaining muscle.

Nutrient Content (Serves 4)

- 286 calories per serving
- 30 g protein
- Carbohydrates: 61g
- 14g fat

Ingredients

- 2 chopped chicken breasts
- 1 chopped onion

- 1 chopped red pepper
- 2 crushed garlic cloves
- 100g sliced chorizo
- 1 tbsp Cajun seasoning
- 250g brown rice
- 1 tbsp olive oil
- 350g chopped tomatoes from a can
- 350ml chicken stock

Procedure

1. In a wide pan, heat the olive oil over medium heat.

2. Add the chicken and cook for about 8 minutes, stirring occasionally. Set to the side.

3. Add the onion to the pan and cook until it is soft and translucent. Cook for about 5 minutes with the garlic, chorizo, Cajun seasoning, and red pepper in the pan.

4. Combine the brown rice, sliced tomatoes, ham, and chicken stock in a pan. Allow to simmer, covered, for about 25 minutes, or until the rice is tender.

POWER PESTO CHICKEN PASTA

To spice things up, try this protein-packed pasta dish!

Nutrient Content (Serves 2)

- 550 calories per serving
- 25 g protein
- Carbohydrates: 30 g
- 19g fat

Ingredients

- 200g grilled chicken breast
- 100g whole-wheat pasta
- 1 tbsp pesto
- A pinch of black pepper
- A handful of basil
- Spinach
- Rocket
- Pine nuts
- Diced tomatoes
- 2 tbsp olive oil

Procedure

1. Bring a big pot of water to a boil over high heat.

2. Toss in the whole-wheat pasta and wait for the water to return to a boil.

3. Lower the heat until the water is barely simmering. Allow 10 minutes for the whole-wheat pasta to cook.

4. In a mixing bowl, combine the pesto, olive oil, and black pepper.

5. Toss in the diced chicken breasts, pine nuts, onions, and herbs.

6. Drain the pasta and fold the mixture into the pan until it is evenly distributed.

SPICY CHICKEN TRAY-BAKE

A delicious chicken recipe that is easy to prepare and contains all of the essential muscle-building nutrients.

Nutrient Content (Serves 4)

- 276 calories per serving
- 40 g protein
- Carbohydrates: 14 g
- 7g fat

Ingredients

- 4 chicken breasts (skinless)
- 250g low-fat natural yogurt
- 3 tablespoons harissa paste
- 1 small butternut squash (peeled and chopped)
- 2 chopped red onions
- 1 tablespoon olive oil

Procedure

1. Preheat the oven to 375°F/190°C/Gas Mark 5 (375°F/190°C/Gas Mark 5).

2. In a mixing bowl, combine 3 tablespoons yogurt and 2 tablespoons harissa. Set aside the chicken breast after coating it with the mixture.

3. In a baking tray, combine the onions, sliced butternut squash, 1 tablespoon harissa, and 2 tablespoons olive oil. Bake for 10 minutes. Remove the tray from the oven and place the chicken breast on it. Return to the oven and cook for another 20 minutes, or until the chicken is thoroughly cooked.

4. Arrange on a plate and top with the yogurt that's left over.

MUSCLE MOROCCAN CHICKEN CASSEROLE

A traditional Moroccan casserole with a lot of protein, a lot of flavor, and very little fat.

Nutrient Content (Serves 4)

- 404 calories per serving
- 47 g protein
- Carbohydrates: 37 g
- 8 g fat

Ingredients

- 4 chicken breasts
- 1 tsp ground cumin
- 1 tsp paprika
- 1 tbsp olive oil
- 1 chopped onion
- 350g canned chopped tomatoes
- 2 tbsp harissa paste
- 1 tbsp honey
- 2 medium thickly sliced courgettes
- 400g drained and rinsed chickpeas

Procedure

1. Season the chicken breasts with salt, pepper, paprika, and ground cumin.

2. Next, pour the olive oil into a wide pan and heat over medium heat.

3. Add the chicken and onions to the pan and cook for four minutes per side on each side.

4. Add the chopped tomatoes and 200ml water to the pan, along with the sugar, harissa, courgettes, and chickpeas, and mix all together.

5. Bring the mixture to a low boil and cook for about 15 minutes.

6. Arrange on a plate and serve.

ANABOLIC RATATOUILLE CHICKEN

A delicious low-carb chicken recipe for muscle gain and fat loss.

Nutrient Content (Serves 4)

- 324 calories per serving
- 38 g protein
- Carbohydrates: 10 g
- 15 g fat

Ingredients

- 4 chicken breasts
- 1 chopped onion
- 2 chopped red peppers
- 1 courgette, cut into chunks
- 1 small aubergine
- cut into chunks
- 4 chopped tomatoes
- 4 tbsp olive oil

Procedure

1. Preheat the oven to 375°F/190°C/Gas Mark 5 (375°F/190°C/Gas Mark 5).

2. Toss all of the vegetables and tomatoes in a tray with 3 tablespoons olive oil.

3. Arrange the chicken breasts on top of the vegetables and season with the remaining tbsp olive oil, salt, and pepper.

4. Bake for about 30 minutes with the tray in the oven.

5. Arrange on a plate and serve

CHICKEN BRAWN BURGER

Another fantastic healthy burger option! If you're short on time, this dish is quick and simple to prepare. It has a lot of protein in it to hold you anabolic.

Nutrient Content

- 458 calories per serving
- 50 g protein
- Carbohydrates: 38 g
- 12 g fat

Ingredients

- 1 breast of chicken
- 1 tbsp low-fat mayonnaise
- 1 chopped red onion
- 1 chopped lettuce

- 1 slice low-fat cheddar
- 1 whole wheat burger bun
- 1 tsp chopped jalapeno slices

Procedure

1. In a griddle pan, heat the olive oil over medium heat.

2. Season the chicken breast with salt and pepper, then place it in the pan and cook for 5 minutes. Cook for another 5 minutes on the other hand.

3. Place the cheddar slice on top of the chicken. Cook for another 8 minutes, or until chicken is thoroughly cooked.

4. Remove the chicken from the pan and set it aside.

5. Toss the chicken, onions, mayonnaise, lettuce, and chopped jalapeno into the open roll.

HONEY GLAZED GROWTH CHICKEN

With this sweet and enticing chicken recipe, you can shake things up a little.

Nutrient Content (Serves 2)

- 195 calories per serving
- 37 g protein
- Carbs: 9g
- 2 g fat

Ingredients

- 2 skinless chicken breasts
- 12 lemon
- 1 tbsp honey
- 1 tbsp dark soy sauce

- seasonings (salt and pepper)

Procedure

1. Preheat the oven to 375°F/190°C/Gas Mark 5 (375°F/190°C/Gas Mark 5).

2. Season the chicken breasts with salt and pepper and place them in a baking dish.

3. Squeeze the lemon juice into a bowl and add the honey and soy sauce. Combine the ingredients and use to coat the chicken breasts.

4. Put the chicken breasts in the oven with the squeezed lemon in between them and cook for about 30 minutes, or until completely cooked through.

BRAWNY CHICKEN CHASSEUR

A delicious and classic chicken dish that's high in protein and low in carbs.

Nutrient Content (Serves 4)

- 242 calories per serving
- 50 g protein
- Carbohydrates: 5 g
- 3 g fat

Ingredients

- 8 chopped turkey bacon rashers
- 4 chopped chicken breasts
- 200g baby mushrooms
- 1 tbsp plain flour
- 400g canned chopped tomatoes
- 1 beef stock cube

- 1 tbsp Worcestershire sauce
- Handful chopped parsley

Procedure

1. In a shallow saucepan, heat the olive oil over medium heat, then add the turkey bacon and cook for 4-5 minutes, or until it begins to brown.

2. Cook for about 5 minutes, or until the chicken breasts are golden. Increase the heat to high and cook for 2 minutes with the baby mushrooms. Stir in the flour until a paste begins to form.

3. Cook for about 10 minutes after adding the canned chopped tomatoes and beef stock cube to the saucepan.

4. Finally, stir in the parsley and Worcestershire sauce before serving.

MIGHTY MEXICAN CHICKEN STEW

This traditional Mexican chicken stew adds some heat to the table. The chicken, as well as the quinoa, are also high in protein.

Nutrient Content (Serves 4)

- 464 calories per serving
- 51 g protein
- Carbohydrates: 53 g
- 4 g fat

Ingredients

- 4 skinless chicken breasts
- 140g quinoa
- 400g drained pinto beans
- 1 tablespoon olive oil
- 1 chopped onion

- 2 chopped red peppers
- 3 tablespoons chipotle paste
- 800g tinned chopped tomatoes
- 2 chicken stock cubes
- 1 lime

Procedure

1. In a deep pan, heat the olive oil over medium heat and cook the onion and peppers for 2-3 minutes.

2. Stir in the chipotle paste and sliced tomatoes from a can.

3. Add the chicken breasts and just enough water to cover them by 1cm, then reduce the heat to low and allow the mixture to simmer. Cook for about 20 minutes, or until the chicken is thoroughly cooked.

4. Place the stock cubes and boiling water in a separate saucepan. Heat for about 12 minutes after adding the quinoa.

5. Cook for another 3 minutes after adding the pinto beans. Drain the quinoa and combine with the coriander and lime juice; blend well and set aside.

6. Toss the chicken with the quinoa and top with the pan tomato sauce.

TASTY TURKEY BAGEL

This is a fantastic meal for lunch or after a workout! It's high in protein, so it'll keep you developing.

Nutrient Content

- 336 calories per serving

- 21 g protein
- Carbohydrates: 64 g
- 1 gram of fat

Ingredients

- 14 sliced cucumber
- 2 thick deli turkey breast slices (cooked)
- 1 whole-wheat bagel
- Handful of baby spinach
- Handful of rocket
- 1 chopped tomato

Procedure

1. Split the whole-wheat bagel in half, then toast each half separately.

2. Toss the bagel with the turkey breast, chopped onion, cucumber, spinach, and rocket.

3. Take it with you or eat it at home!

SPICY CAJUN CHICKEN WITH GUACAMOLE

Delicious low-carb, low-fat chicken recipe! It has a high protein content to keep you building muscle and burning fat.

Nutrient Content (Serves 4)

- 190 calories per serving
- 34 g protein
- Carbohydrates: 2 g
- 5 g fat

Ingredients

- 1 tbsp paprika
- 4 chicken breasts
- 1 tbsp olive oil
- 200g guacamole
- 1 tsp dried onion flakes
- 14 tsp cayenne pepper
- 2 tsp dried thyme
- A pinch of salt and pepper

Procedure

1. In a mixing bowl, combine the cayenne pepper, dried thyme, paprika, salt, pepper, and onion flakes.

2. Cut two deep scores in each breast of the chicken. The chicken should be rubbed with oil before the spices are applied to the breasts.

3. Place the chicken on the grill and cook for 8 minutes on each side, or until fully cooked.

4. Toss the chicken with the guacamole and serve.

AESTHETIC TOMATO AND OLIVE PAN-FRIED CHICKEN

A delicious chicken dish that will fulfill both your appetite and your nutritional needs.

Nutrient Content (Serves 2)

- 334 calories per serving
- 39 g protein

- Carbohydrates: 8 g
- 19g fat

Ingredients

2 chicken breasts, 1 chopped onion, 2 chopped garlic cloves, 400g canned chopped tomatoes, 1 tbsp balsamic vinegar, 6 chopped green olives, 300ml chicken stock, 2 tbsp olive oil, a pinch of salt and pepper

Procedure

1. In a pan, heat the olive oil over medium heat.

2. Season the chicken with salt and pepper before placing it in the pan and cooking for about 10 minutes, or until the chicken is cooked through.

3. Add the onion to the pan and cook for another 4–5 minutes before flipping the chicken. Take the chicken out of the pan and set it aside.

4. Stir in the garlic and proceed to cook the onions until they are tender.

5. Add the chopped tomatoes, olives, chicken stock, and balsamic vinegar to the pan, along with the majority of the basil leaves, and cook for around 8 minutes on low heat.

6. Return the chicken to the pan, cover, and cook for another 5 minutes.

7. Arrange on plates and top with the remaining basil.

MUSCLE CHICKEN CACCIATORE

A delicious, low-fat, low-carb chicken recipe with an Italian flair. It has a lot of protein in it, so you'll be able to keep building muscle and burning fat.

Nutrient Content (Serves 4)

- 172 calories per serving
- 33 g protein
- Carbohydrates: 6 g
- 2 g fat

Ingredients

- 4 chicken breasts
- 1 chopped onion
- 2 sliced garlic cloves
- 1 tsp olive oil
- 400g tinned chopped tomatoes
- 2 tbsp chopped rosemary leaves
- Handful of basil leaves

Procedure

1. Preheat the oven to 375°F/190°C/Gas Mark 5 (375°F/190°C/Gas Mark 5).

2. In a medium-sized pan, heat the oil and cook the onion and garlic until tender.

3. Add the chopped tomatoes, rosemary, salt, and pepper, and cook for about 15 minutes, or until the sauce has thickened.

4. Spread the mixture over the chicken, put it on a baking sheet, and bake it. Place the chicken in the oven for 20 minutes, or until it is fully cooked. Serve the chicken with a basil sprig on top.

DICED CHICKEN WITH EGG NOODLES

Don't be afraid to shake things up with this delectable recipe. It has the right balance of protein, carbohydrates, and fats to help you achieve your goals.

Nutrient Content (Serves 2)

- 322 calories per serving
- 30 g protein
- Carbohydrates: 31 g
- 8 g fat

Ingredients

- 150 g chicken breast, chopped
- 1 grated carrot
- 2 tbsp fresh orange juice
- 1 tsp sesame seeds
- 3 tbsp soy sauce
- 2 tbsp rapeseed oil
- 1 chopped ginger
- 100g sugar snap peas

Procedure

1. In a medium-sized pan, heat 1 tablespoon rapeseed oil.

2. Cook the chopped chicken breast for 10-15 minutes, or until it is completely cooked.

3. Cook the noodles in a pot of boiling water for about 5 minutes while the chicken is cooking.

4. Combine the ginger, sesame seeds, soy sauce, 1 tablespoon rapeseed oil, and orange juice in a mixing bowl.

CHAPTER 6: RED MEAT AND PORK

ORIENTAL BEEF MUSCLE STIR-FRY

Great beef recipe that's high in protein to keep you rising and losing weight.

Nutrient Content (Serves 4)

- 349 calories per serving
- 34 g protein
- Carbohydrates: 26 g
- 14g fat

Ingredients

- 1 tsp Chinese five-spice powder
- 500g diced beef rump
- 300g egg noodles
- 1 big chopped red chili
- 1 garlic clove
- 1 thumb-size piece of ginger chopped
- 1 stick lemongrass
- 2 tbsp olive oil

- 100g sugar snap peas
- 8 baby corns, sliced diagonally
- 6 chopped spring onions
- 12 lime
- 2 tbsp soy sauce
- 1 tablespoon of fish sauce
- 2 tbsp roasted peanuts
- To eat, a pinch of chopped coriander

Procedure

1. In a mixing bowl, combine the beef and five-spice powder and set aside to marinate. Cook the egg noodles in a pot of boiling water for 5 minutes, then drain and set aside.

2. In a mixing bowl, combine the chopped chilli, ginger, garlic, and lemongrass.

3. Heat 1 tablespoon olive oil in a wok over medium heat. Fry for 1 minute in the wok with the ginger mixture. Increase the heat to high and add 1 tbsp olive oil to the wok, then add the beef and cook until browned.

4. Stir-fry the sugar snaps, spring onions, and baby corn in the wok for about a minute before adding the egg noodles and mixing it together. Remove the pan from the heat and stir in the soy sauce, fish sauces, and lime juice.

5. To eat, place in a bowl with the peanuts and chopped coriander.

MASS GAINING LAMB FLATBREAD

A delicious and nutritious homemade flatbread with a Moroccan twist, with plenty of protein to keep you and your muscles fueled!

Nutrient Content (Serves 4)

- 391 calories per serving
- 29 g protein
- Carbohydrates: 34 g
- 17g fat

Ingredients

- 2 200g lamb leg steaks
- 1 tbsp harissa
- 4 whole meal flatbreads
- 4 tbsp organic houmous
- Handful of baby spinach
- Handful of watercress

Procedure

1. Prepare the grill by preheating it.

2. Season the lamb with harissa, salt, and pepper.

3. Place the lamb on a baking sheet and grill for 4 minutes before flipping it and cooking for another 4 minutes. Remove the tray from the grill and set it aside.

4. Grill the flatbreads for 1–2 minutes before removing them and spreading the houmous on top.

5. Slice the lamb into thin strips and spread them on top of the flatbread.

TASTY BEEF BROCCOLI STIR FRY

This healthy beef stir-fry is fast and simple to make, and it will save you money on Chinese takeout!

Nutrient Content (Serves 4)

- 277 calories per serving
- 30 g protein
- Carbohydrates: 7 g
- 14g fat

Ingredients

- 400g diced frying beef steaks
- 1 head of broccoli, split into florets
- 4 chopped celery sticks
- Handful of sweet corn
- 150ml beef stock
- 2 tbsp horseradish sauce
- 1 tbsp olive oil

Procedure

1. In a frying pan, heat the olive oil over medium/high heat.

2. Season the beefsteaks with salt and pepper before placing them in the frying pan.

3. Cook for 2 minutes, or until the beef is browned, then remove from the pan and set aside.

4. Add the broccoli and celery to the pan and continue to cook for another 2 minutes.

5. Pour in the beef stock and cover the pan. Reduce the heat to low and continue to cook the vegetables for another 2 minutes.

6. Return the steak to the pan and stir in the remaining vegetables for another minute.

7. Arrange on a plate and top with horseradish sauce.

SUPER STEAK WITH SPICY RICE & BEANS

The ideal steak...

Nutrient Content (Serves 2)

- 650 calories per serving
- 48 g protein
- Carbohydrates: 60 g
- 26 g fat

Ingredients

- 2 250g sirloin steaks
- 4 tbsp olive oil
- 1 small onion, sliced
- 100g brown long-grain rice
- 112tsp fajita seasoning
- 1 can of drained kidney beans
- Handful of chopped coriander leaves

Procedure

1. In a deep saucepan over medium heat, pour 3 tsp oil and add the onion. For about 4 minutes, fry the onion.

2. Toss in 12 tbsp. fajita seasoning and 12 tbsp. long grain rice. 1 minute of cooking Stir in 300ml of boiling water to the saucepan. Cover the saucepan and cook for 20 minutes, or until the rice is fluffy and the water has been absorbed. Keep the kidney beans warm in the pan.

3. Season the steak with salt and pepper, as well as 12 fajita seasoning, while the rice is cooking. Pre-heat a griddle pan over high heat, then add the steaks and cook for an additional 8 minutes, turning halfway through.

4. Combine the rice and coriander in a mixing dish. Serve with a tablespoon of tomato salsa on each steak.

BULK-UP LAMB CURRY & PEANUT STEW

This curry is flavorful and filling, with a good amount of protein to boot.

Nutrient Content (Serves 4)

- 600 calories per serving
- 44 g protein
- Carbohydrates: 38 g
- 46 g fat

Ingredients

- 600g diced lamb steak (or beef)
- 450g chopped white potatoes
- 1 chopped onion
- 1 cinnamon stick
- 1 tbsp tamarind paste
- 1 tbsp fish sauce
- 50g chopped peanuts
- 400ml canned coconut cream

- 4 tbsp massaman curry paste
- 1 red chili, sliced

Procedure

1. Preheat the oven to 375°F/190°C/Gas Mark 5 (375°F/190°C/Gas Mark 5).

2. Preheat the oven to 350°F and put a large casserole dish on the stovetop over medium heat.

3. Cook for about a minute with 2 tbsp coconut cream and the curry paste before adding the diced lamb. Brown after stirring in. Add the rest of the coconut milk, as well as the potatoes, onions, cinnamon stick, tamarind, fish sauce, and peanuts, along with a cup of water.

4. Lower the heat to a low simmer, cover the casserole, and bake for 2 hours, or until the lamb is soft and tender.

5. Garnish with sliced chilli and serve.

MUSCLE MINT LAMB STEAKS

Delicious recipe with over 40 grams of protein to keep you muscle-building and fat-burning!

Nutrient Ccontent (Serves 2)

- 367 calories per serving
- 41 g protein
- Carbohydrates: 2 g
- 22g fat

Ingredients

- 4 200g lamb leg steaks

- 2 tbsp olive oil
- 2 chopped garlic cloves
- 1 tbsp balsamic vinegar
- Handful of chopped mint leaves

Procedure

1. Combine the mint, vinegar, and garlic in a mixing bowl.

2. Place the lamb in the bowl with the marinade and leave for at least 30 minutes.

3. Preheat a griddle pan to medium-high heat and cook the lamb for 4 minutes on each side or until completely cooked.

4. Serve alone or with a salad of your choosing for a delectable side dish.

ANABOLIC PORK SOUP

This soup is easy to make and high in protein, which helps to create muscle and burn fat.

Nutrient Content (Serves 4)

- 297 calories per serving
- 21 g protein
- Carbohydrates: 13 g
- 17g fat

Ingredients

- 400g diced pork steaks
- 600ml chicken stock
- 1 tablespoon soy sauce
- 2 tsp Chinese five-spice powder
- 25g finely chopped ginger
- 200g baby spinach kit

- 1 tsp chopped red chilli
- 200g rice noodles
- Handful chopped spring onions

Procedure

1. Combine all of the ingredients in a big saucepan, except the spring onions and noodles. On a medium heat, cover the pan and bring to a simmer.

2. Cook for about 8-10 minutes without allowing the ingredients to boil.

3. Cook the rice noodles in a pot of boiling water for about 5 minutes while the pork is frying.

4. Drain the noodles and put them in a mixing bowl with the pork and greens. Serve with a sprinkling of spring onions on top.

SUPER LAMB STEAKS WITH MEDITERRANEAN VEG

A lamb dish with a Mediterranean twist! A fast and simple lamb recipe that will keep you going for longer...

Nutrient Content (Serves 2)

- 308 calories per serving
- 34 g protein
- Carbohydrates: 15 g
- 14g fat

Ingredients

- 2 200g lamb leg/breast steaks
- 2 chopped courgettes
- 2 tbsp olive oil
- Handful of rocket
- 2 chopped garlic cloves

- 8 halved baby cherry tomatoes

Procedure

1. Prepare the grill by preheating it.

2. Heat the oil in a skillet over medium heat.

3. Add the courgettes, tomatoes, and garlic and cook until the tomatoes and courgettes are tender.

4. Stir in the rocket and coriander leaves.

5. Meanwhile, season the lamb steaks with salt and pepper. Grill the lamb for 4 minutes on either side on a plate.

6. Serve with the vegetables.

BRAWNY BEEF FAJITAS

Fast and simple beef recipe that's great for lunch and high in protein to keep you rising and burning calories.

Nutrient Content

- 358 calories per serving
- 28 g protein
- Carbohydrates: 40 g
- 10 g fat

Ingredients

- 1 wholegrain fajita wrap
- 2 tbsp sweet chilli sauce
- 100g diced lean steak
- 1 chopped red onion
- 1 chopped red pepper

Procedure

1. In a pan, stir fry the diced steak, chopped onion, red pepper, and 1 tbsp chilli sauce for 4–5 minutes on a medium to high heat.

2. Microwave the wrap for 30 seconds or cook it on the grill for the same period of time.

3. Toss the fajita with the steak mixture and a tbsp of sweet chili sauce.

4. Enjoy it!

STRENGTH AND MASS MEATLOAF

The ideal meatloaf for gaining muscle mass!

Nutrient Content (Serves 6)

- 410 calories per serving
- 47 g protein
- Carbohydrates: 15 g
- 19g fat

Ingredients

- 1 tsp olive oil
- 1 chopped red onion
- 1 tsp garlic
- 3 chopped tomatoes
- 1 whole beaten egg
- 100g whole wheat bread crumbs
- Handful of parsley

- 20g low fat parmesan
- 50ml organic skim milk
- A pinch of salt and pepper
- 1 tsp oregano

Procedure

1. Preheat the oven to 400°F/200°C/Gas Mark 6 (400°F/200°C/Gas Mark 6).

2. Heat the oil in a skillet over medium heat.

3. Saute the onions until they are soft but not browned. Allow the onions to cool after removing them from the pan.

4. In a large mixing bowl, combine all of the ingredients.

5. Place the meat in a large baking tray and bake for 30-35 minutes at high heat.

6. Serve when the chicken is fully cooked and piping hot.

POWER PORK FRUIT TRAY

This dish is one of my favorites when it comes to pork recipes. For those of you who are shredding, it has a lot of protein and is low in carbs.

Nutrient Content (Serves 4)

- 335 calories per serving
- 42 g protein
- Carbohydrates: 12 g
- 14g fat

Ingredients

- 4 pork steaks

- 1 tablespoon olive oil
- 2 diced red onions
- 2 sliced broad pears
- 3 rosemary sprigs
- 50g diced blue cheese
- 1 diced courgette
- A sprinkle of salt and pepper
- A handful of pine nuts

Procedure

1. Heat the olive oil in a wide pan over medium heat.

2. Combine the courgette, red onions, sliced pears, and salt and pepper in a mixing bowl.

3. Cook for about 6 minutes, or until the vegetables begin to caramelize.

4. Prepare the grill by preheating it.

5. Get a baking tray and place the ingredients in it, along with the rosemary sprigs. Season the pork steaks with salt and pepper before placing them in the tray.

6. Place the tray in the oven and cook for 10-15 minutes, or until the pork steaks are cooked through, turning halfway through. Enable the cheese to melt for another 4-5 minutes after adding the pine nuts.

7. Arrange on a plate and eat.

FARLEY'S MUSCLE BUILDING CHILLI CON CARNE

Chilli con carne is a dish that everybody enjoys. This healthier version, on the other hand, will provide you with over 30 grams of protein and a smug sense of accomplishment!

Nutrient Content (Serves 4)

- 389 calories per serving
- 37 g protein
- Carbohydrates: 25 g
- 17g fat

Ingredients

- 1 tbsp oil
- 1 chopped onion
- 1 chopped red pepper
- 2 crushed garlic cloves
- 1 tsp chilli powder
- 400g of tinned sliced tomatoes
- 2 tbsp tomato purée
- 400g of dried and rinsed red kidney beans
- 100g of brown rice
- 1 tsp paprika
- 1 tsp ground cumin
- 1 beef stock cube

Procedure

1. Pour the olive oil into a pan and heat over medium heat.

2. Toss in the onions and cook until tender.

3. Add the garlic, red pepper, chili powder, paprika, and cumin after that. Cook for 5 minutes after stirring all together.

4. Cook until the ground mince is browned in the pan.

5. Boil 300 mL of water and dissolve the beef stock cube in it. Combine this with the chopped tomatoes in the pan. Also, apply the puree and thoroughly mix it in. Cook

for about 50 minutes after bringing the pan to a boil and covering it. Stir once in a while.

6. After 30 minutes, when the mince is cooking, fill a separate pot halfway with cold water and bring to a boil. When the water is boiling, add the rice and cook for 20 minutes.

7. When the rice is finished, drain it and set it aside. Cook for another 10 minutes after adding the beans to the meat mixture.

8. Toss the rice with the chili con carne and serve.

MIGHTY LAMB CASSEROLE

This meal is both delicious and simple to prepare.

Nutrient Content (Serves 2)

- 380 calories per serving
- 35 g protein
- Carbohydrates: 33 g
- 9 g fat

Ingredients

- 1 tbsp olive oil
- 2 cubed lamb fillets
- 1 chopped onion
- 2 thickly sliced chopped carrots
- Handful of kale
- 400ml chicken stock
- 1 tsp dried rosemary

- 1 tsp chopped parsley
- 400g rinsed and drained cannellini beans

Procedure

1. Heat the olive oil in a large casserole dish over medium heat.

2. Brown the lamb in the casserole dish for 5 minutes before adding the chopped onion and carrots. Cook for another 5 minutes, or until the vegetables have softened.

3. Combine the chicken stock, kale, and rosemary in a large mixing bowl. Cover the casserole and cook on a low heat for 1-1.5 hours, or until the lamb is tender and thoroughly cooked.

4. 15 minutes before the end of the cooking time, add the cannellini beans.

5. Arrange on plates and top with chopped parsley.

BRAWNY BEEF SANDWICHES

Making your own sandwiches is not only cheaper but much healthier than buying them from the store. This meaty sandwich will keep you anabolic for a long time.

Nutrient Content

- 545 calories per serving
- 43 g protein
- Carbohydrates: 64 g
- 10 g fat

Ingredients

- 4 slices deli beef
- 4 slices whole-wheat bread
- 2 teaspoons mustard
- A handful of baby spinach leaves
- 1/2 sliced cucumber
- A pinch of black pepper

Procedure

1. Cut two slices of bread in half.

2. Make a sandwich with 2 slices of deli beef, 1 teaspoon mustard, 12 slices of cucumber, spinach, and a pinch of black pepper.

3. Carry on with the rest of the ingredients in the same manner.

MUSCLE BUILDING STEAK & SWEET POTATO FRIES

A delicious and nutritious alternative to traditional steak and chips! It's high in protein and slow-release carbohydrates.

Nutrient Content (Serves 4)

- 418 calories per serving
- 29 g protein
- Carbohydrates: 39 g
- 15 g fat

Ingredients

- 200g sweet potatoes sliced into chips
- 100g sirloin steak
- 1 tablespoon olive oil
- 1 diced red onion

- 1 pre-washed salad bag
- 1 tablespoon balsamic vinegar
- A pinch of black pepper

Procedure

1. Preheat the oven to 375°F/190°C/Gas Mark 5 (375°F/190°C/Gas Mark 5).

2. Spread the chips out on a baking tray and bake for about 25 minutes.

3. While the chips are cooking, heat the olive oil in a large frying pan over medium heat.

4. Season the steaks with salt and pepper and place them in the pan. Fry the steaks for a total of 6 minutes, turning once halfway through.

5. Remove the steak and set it aside to cool.

6. Toss the salad with the chopped onion in a big mixing bowl. Serve with the potatoes and steak, drizzled with the vinegar.

STEAK & CHEESE MUSCLE CLUB

An incredibly nutritious homemade sandwich with plenty of protein to keep you building muscle and burning fat.

Nutrient Content (Serves 2)

- 336 calories per serving
- 32 g protein
- Carbohydrates: 27 g
- 11g fat

Ingredients

- 1 250g sirloin steak
- 2 whole-meal bread rolls
- 1 tsp olive oil
- 1 tsp Dijon mustard
- Handful of rocket
- 30g Stilton cheese
- 1 tsp balsamic vinegar

Procedure

1. Preheat a griddle pan over high heat until it is extremely hot. Drizzle the olive oil all over the steak, including both sides. Season the steak with salt and pepper, then put it in the pan and cook for 3 minutes on each side. Place the steak to the side and set aside for a minute to rest.

2. Cut the steak in half to make two slices.

3. Toast the whole-wheat rolls by cutting them in half. When the steak is cooked, spread the mustard and rocket on the roll and cover with one half of the steak. Top with balsamic vinegar and cheese, then assemble the sandwich.

4. Do the same thing with the other roll.

CHAPTER 7: FISH & SEAFOOD

STRENGTHENING SUB-CONTINENTAL SARDINES

Sardines are high in protein and omega-3 fatty acids.

Nutrient Content (Serves 4)

- 356 calories per serving
- 20 g protein
- Carbohydrates: 52 g
- 7g fat

Ingredients

- 50g pure flour
- 10 scaled and washed sardines (8 if large)
- 2 whole lemons' zest
- Handful of chopped flat-leaf parsley
- 3 garlic cloves, finely chopped
- 3 tablespoons olive oil

- 400g tinned chopped tomatoes
- 800g chickpeas or butterbeans, drained and rinsed
- 250g pack cherry tomatoes, halved

Procedure

1. Season the flour with salt and pepper before spreading it out on the work surface.

2. Dust all sides of the sardines with flour.

3. In a separate cup, combine the lemon zest, chopped parsley (reserve a pinch for garnish), and half of the chopped garlic.

4. Preheat the grill to high and place a very large pan on it.

5. When the oil is very hot, add the floured sardines and lay them flat.

6. Fry for 3 minutes on one side until golden brown, then flip and fry for another 3 minutes. Place these on a plate to cool.

7. Fry the remaining garlic for 1 minute, until softened (add more oil if necessary). Pour in the chopped tomato tin, stir well, and cook for 4-5 minutes.

8. Stir in the chickpeas or butter beans, as well as the fresh tomatoes, until thoroughly cooked.

9. Add the sardines to the lemon and parsley mixture and cook for an additional 3-4 minutes.

10. Garnish with a pinch of parsley until they've finished cooking.

STEAMY WORKOUT FISH

This dish is light and refreshing; it's easy to prepare and can be loaded with extra greens and vitamins!

Nutrient Content

Servings calorie count per serving: 4 145 words

- 29 g protein
- Carbohydrates: 4 g
- 1 gram of fat

Ingredients

- Baking sheets, greaseproof paper, or tin foil
- 100g pak choi
- 4 x 150g solid white fish fillets (Cod, Plaice, Pollock, Seabass, or Haddock)
- 2 garlic cloves, finely chopped
- 1 tsp rice wine mirin
- Handful of chopped coriander
- 4 chopped spring onion stems

Procedure

1. Preheat the oven to 200°C/400°F/Gas Mark 6 (200°C/400°F/Gas Mark 6).

2. You'll need tin foil, greaseproof paper, or baking paper to create a parcel for your delectable ingredients.

3. Cut four wide rectangles from the paper and put each fillet on one of them.

4. Combine the garlic, soy sauce, and rice wine in a mixing bowl.

5. You may want to squeeze the juices into your parcel with one or two lime wedges.

6. Make a parcel out of these by folding one edge open.

7. After cooking for 20 minutes, add the spring onions and chilli for a fresh finish.

PROTEIN PACKED PAELLA

A tasty, traditional Spanish dish with plenty of flavor and protein to keep you building muscle and burning fat.

Nutrient Content (Serves 4)

- 351 calories per serving
- 21 g protein
- Carbohydrates: 50 g
- 9 g fat

Ingredients

- 200g cooked frozen prawns
- 2 diced chorizo sausages
- 1 tbsp olive oil
- 1 chopped onion
- 1 chopped garlic clove
- 12 tsp turmeric
- 600g brown rice
- 100g frozen peas

Procedure

1. In a large skillet, heat the olive oil over high heat. Fry for 2-3 minutes, until the chorizo, onion, and garlic are tender.

2. Combine the turmeric, rice, prawns, and frozen peas with 100 mL boiling water.

3. Continue stirring until the mixture is warm and the water has been absorbed.

4. Arrange on a plate and eat.

MUSCLE BUILDING SARDINES ON TOAST

A simple muscle-building recipe that is ideal for lunches or snacks.

Nutrient Content (Serves 2)

- 442 calories per serving
- 24 g protein
- Carbohydrates: 30 g
- 23g fat

Ingredients

- 4 slices Ezekiel bread or whole wheat brown bread
- 2 cans drained sardines in olive oil
- 1 tablespoon olive oil
- 1 chopped garlic clove
- 1 chopped red chili
- 1 lemon, zest and juice

Procedure

1. Start by toasting the bread.

2. In a medium-sized pan, heat some olive oil.

3. Add the chilli, garlic, lemon zest, and sardines to the pan and cook for 2-3 minutes, or until the sardines are cooked.

4. Arrange the sardines on the toast and garnish with parsley. To serve, drizzle a few drops of lemon juice on top.

MIGHTY TUNA MELTS

Are you stumped as to what to do with the tuna can stashed in the back of the pantry? This is a delicious protein-packed recipe that takes just a few minutes to prepare.

Nutrient Content (Serves 2)

- 450 calories per serving
- 37 g protein
- Carbohydrates: 20 g
- 24 g fat

Ingredients

- 200g tinned, drained tuna
- 2 sliced spring onion stems
- 4 tbsp low-fat mayonnaise
- 4 thick slices Ezekial or wholemeal bread
- 50g grated low fat cheddar
- 2 tbsp chilli flakes
- 1 squeezed lemon

Procedure

1. Preheat the grill and toast the bread.

2. In a mixing bowl, combine the spring onions, mayonnaise, tuna, and chilli flakes, as well as the salt, pepper, and lemon juice. Combine all of the ingredients.

3. Spread the tuna mixture on top of the bread slices, then sprinkle with grated cheese. Place the cheese under the grill until it begins to bubble.

4. Arrange on a plate and eat.

TASTY TUNA, BROCCOLI & CAULIFLOWER PASTA BAKE

For both your muscle-building and fat-loss needs, this delicious pasta meal is filled with protein.

Nutrient Content (Serves 4)

- 641 calories per serving
- 37 g protein
- Carbohydrates: 73 g
- 22g fat

Ingredients

- 2 cans tuna in olive oil (drained)
- 800g canned chopped tomatoes
- 350g whole-wheat pasta
- 150g chopped broccoli
- 150g chopped cauliflower
- 200g light soft cheese
- 100g grated cheddar
- 25g whole-wheat breadcrumbs

Procedure

1. Heat the olive oil in a pan over medium/high heat.

2. Add the canned tomatoes and 200ml of water to the pot and bring to a boil.

3. Bring a large pot of water to a boil in another large pan. Wait until the pan begins to boil again before adding the whole-wheat pasta. Reduce the heat to a low setting until the water is barely simmering. Allow 10 minutes for the whole-wheat

pasta to cook. During the last 3 minutes of cooking, add the broccoli and cauliflower, then drain.

4. Preheat the grill while the pasta and vegetables are cooking.

5. Whisk in the cheese until it melts into the tomato sauce, then add the drained pasta, tomatoes, and tuna.

6. Transfer the mixture to a deep baking dish and top with the cheddar, breadcrumbs, salt, and pepper.

7. Place under the grill for 6 minutes, or until golden brown.

8. Arrange on a plate and eat.

MUSCLE MACKEREL AND SPICY COUSCOUS

Mackerel is a high-protein, low-fat fish that is also high in omega-3 fatty acids.

Nutrient Content

- 484 calories per serving
- 26 g protein
- Carbohydrates: 35 g
- 26 g fat

Ingredients

- 150g couscous
- 100g precooked mackerel
- 1 tsp ground cumin
- 1 tsp smoked paprika
- 1 chopped red chilli
- pinch of black pepper

- 2 chopped tomatoes
- 1 chopped onion

Procedure

1. Toss the couscous with the cumin, smoked paprika, and a pinch of black pepper in a mixing bowl. Then, pour a cup of boiling water over the couscous until it is covered by around 1cm. Cover the bowl with plastic wrap and set aside for 10-15 minutes.

2. Stir in the chopped chilli, chopped tomatoes, chopped mint, and chopped onion until the water has been absorbed.

3. Top with the mackerel and serve.

BRAWNY BAKED HADDOCK WITH SPINACH AND PEA RISOTTO

Haddock is warm and wholesome filler that is inexpensive and simple to prepare. It is also high in nutrients.

Nutrient Content (Serves 4)

- 469 calories per serving
- 32 g protein
- Carbohydrates: 66 g
- 10 g fat

Ingredients

- 400g smoked haddock (skinless, boneless) from your nearest fishmonger or supermarket
- 1 tbsp olive oil
- 1 chopped onion

- 300g risotto rice
- 450 ml vegetable stock
- 250g fresh spinach leaves
- Handful of frozen peas
- 3 tbsp crème fraîche
- 50g grated parmesan cheese

Procedure

1. In a big pan or wok, heat the oil over medium heat.

2. Fry the chopped onion until it is soft (but not brown), then add the rice and stir until it is soft.

3. Pour in half of the stock and continue to mix slowly until the rice becomes translucent.

4. Continue to slowly add the rest of the stock while stirring for another 20-30 minutes.

5. Add the spinach and peas to the risotto and mix well.

6. Arrange the fish on top of the rice, cover with the lid, and steam for 10 minutes.

7. Flake the fish into big chunks and combine with the crème fraîche and half of the parmesan in a mixing bowl.

8. Season with freshly ground pepper, then top with the remaining parmesan cheese to taste!

RUSTIC SCALLOPS WITH CORIANDER AND LIME

Scallops are a delicacy and, if you're feeling adventurous, a delicious change of pace!

Nutrient Content

- 225 calories per serving
- 20 g protein
- Carbohydrates: 3 g
- 14g fat

Ingredients

- 8 queen or king scallops (row on)
- 1 tablespoon olive oil
- 2 big chopped garlic cloves
- 1 teaspoon chopped fresh red chilli
- 1/2 lime juice
- 2 tablespoons chopped coriander

Procedure

1. Preheat the pan to medium-high heat and fry the scallops for around 1 minute on each side, or until golden brown. Squeeze the lime juice over the scallops and add the chopped chilli and garlic cloves to the pan.

2. To serve, remove the scallops from the pan and top them with the chilli and coriander, as well as some salt and pepper.

SUPER HUMAN SEA BASS WITH SIZZLING SPICES

A tasty meaty meal with high protein content.

Nutrient Content (Serves 6)

- 202 calories per serving
- 28 g protein
- Carbohydrates: 2 g
- 9 g fat

Ingredients

- 6 x skin-on, scaled sea bass fillets
- 3 tbsp olive oil
- 1 thumb-size piece of peeled and chopped ginger
- 3 thinly sliced garlic cloves
- 3 deseeded and thinly sliced red chillies
- 5 sliced spring onion stems
- 1 tbsp soy sauce

Procedure

1. In a wide pan, heat 2 tablespoons of oil over medium heat.

2. Season the Sea Bass with salt and pepper and score the skin of the fish with a sharp knife a few times.

3. Place the sea bass fillet skin side down in a very hot bath (you must press the fish down onto the pan with your cooking spatula to prevent the fish from shrivelling and shrinking).

4. Cook the fish in this manner for about 5 minutes, or until the skin underneath begins to turn golden brown (you should let go of the spatula pressure after the first few seconds)!

5. Flip the fish over for about 30 seconds to get a good golden color on the flesh.

6. Remove the fish from the pan and set it aside.

7. Pour in the remaining oil, along with the chillies, garlic, and ginger, and cook for about 2 minutes, or until golden.

8. Remove from the heat and stir in the spring onions and soy sauce. To make a tasty oriental treat, pour the sauce over the sea bass.

COD AND VEG

A basic recipe that is both fast and easy to prepare and delicious. It's rich in protein and low in carbohydrates, as you may have guessed.

Nutrient Content

- 324 calories per serving
- 28 g protein
- Carbohydrates: 11 g
- 19g fat

Ingredients

- 1 tbsp olive oil
- 2 sliced spring onions
- 1 chopped gem lettuce
- 2 tbsp reduced-fat crème fraîche
- 140g boneless white fish fillet
- Handful frozen peas
- A pinch of salt and pepper
- 1 tbsp reduced-fat crème fraîche

Procedure

1. In a microwave-safe cup, combine the lettuce, spring onions, frozen peas, and olive oil.

2. Season the fish with salt and pepper, as well as 1 tablespoon of crème fraîche, and place it in the mixing bowl.

3. Put the bowl in the microwave after covering it with cling film and piercing it multiple times with a fork.

4. Microwave the bowl for 8 minutes, or until the fish is completely cooked and piping hot all the way through.

5. Remove the fish from the microwave bowl and set it to the side.

6. Mash the vegetables with a fork and serve with the fish and a spoonful of crème fraîche on top.

JOCK'S JACKET POTATO WITH TUNA

Who says a jacket potato has to be uninteresting? If you try this sweet potato version, you'll be happy and complete, with plenty of protein!

Nutrient Content

- 352 calories per serving
- 33 g protein
- Carbohydrates: 27 g
- 13 g fat

Ingredients

- 12 finely chopped red onion
- 1 tiny deseeded and chopped red chilli (dried chilli will suffice)
- 1 tbsp natural yoghurt

- A bunch of spring onions, chopped

Procedure

1. Preheat the oven to 200°C/400°F/Gas Mark 6 (200°C/400°F/Gas Mark 6).

2. You don't have to peel the sweet potato, but you might want to use a sharp knife to scrape off the nobly bits!

3. Prick the potato several times with a fork and microwave for 20 minutes (if you don't have a microwave, use the oven, but it will take about 30 minutes).

4. Season the tuna with salt and pepper when it's cooking by mixing it with the chopped onion and chill.

5. Bake the sweet potato for a further 5-10 minutes, or until slightly crisped, and serve with the tuna mixture and yoghurt on top.

6. Finish with a sprinkling of chopped spring onion!

TRAINING TILAPIA IN THAI SAUCE

Tilapia can sound exotic, but it's a common fish found at your neighborhood fishmonger or supermarket counter. In the event that this isn't possible, you can substitute Sea Bass or any other fish fillets of your choosing!

Nutrient Content (Serves 4)

- 328 calories per serving
- 28 g protein
- Carbohydrates: 25 g
- 14g fat

Ingredients

- 4 tilapia fillets
- 2 tablespoons rice
- 2 tablespoons olive oil
- 4 spring onion stems, diced
- 1 stick chopped lemon grass
- 2 crushed garlic cloves
- 1 thumb-size piece chopped fresh ginger
- 2 tablespoons soy sauce
- 1 lime juice
- plus 1 lime wedged to serve
- 1 minced red chili
- Handful of coriander leaves

Procedure

1. Coat the tilapia fillets in flour, ensuring that the whole fillet is covered.

2. In a medium to high heat pan, add olive oil and fry the fillets for 3 minutes on each side.

3. In the same pan, fry the garlic, chili, lemongrass, and ginger over low heat until fragrant, then add the soy sauce and lime juice and simmer until the sauce thickens slightly.

4. Spoon the sauce over the fish and cook for a few minutes with the spring onions before serving with your choice of herb and lime wedges on the side.

LEMONY SALMON

Salmon is rich in omega 3 fats and a good source of protein. The majority of salmon dishes are bland and dull... This isn't it!

Nutrient Content (Serves 4)

- 205 calories per serving
- 20 g protein
- 1 gram of carbohydrates
- 13 g fat

Ingredients

- 4 100g salmon fillets
- 1 lemon
- 1 minced garlic clove
- A sprinkle of salt and pepper
- 10g chopped tarragon
- A handful of rocket
- 2 tbsp olive oil

Procedure

1. Preheat the grill. Toss together the chopped garlic, tarragon, salt, pepper, and olive oil in a mixing bowl. In a large mixing bowl, squeeze the lemon juice and zest together.

2. Toss the salmon fillets in the marinade in a mixing bowl. Cover the bowl and set aside for 10 minutes to marinate the salmon fillets.

3. Remove the salmon fillets from the bowl and put them on a plate, pouring the marinade over them.

4. Cook the salmon fillets on the grill for about 10 minutes, or until finished.

5. Arrange on a plate and eat.

TANGY TROUT

Trout are the kings of all river fish, and their deliciousness cannot be overstated! Don't rule out sea trout because it's just as beautiful!

Nutrient Content

- 298 calories per serving
- 30 g protein
- Carbohydrates: 10 g
- 16g fat

Ingredients

- 50g whole wheat/brown breadcrumbs (you can buy these pre-packaged or just use your trusty blender to whiz up your crust ends!)
- 4 trout fillets
- 25g toasted and chopped pine nuts or walnuts
- 1 tbsp olive oil
- 1 tiny chopped bunch parsley
- 1 lemon's zest and juice

Procedure

1. Preheat your grill to high heat.

2. Meanwhile, brush a baking tray with oil and combine the breadcrumbs, parsley, lemon zest and juice, and half of the nuts.

3. Place the fillets skin side down on your tray and rub both sides of the fillets into the mixture before drizzling with more olive oil.

4. Place them under the grill for 5 minutes, then top with the remaining nuts to serve.

CHAPTER 8: SALADS

SPICY MEXICAN BEAN STEW

While this is technically a salad, it would be welcome on any dinner table. You won't go hungry after this one, and the heat will definitely get your metabolism going!

Nutrient Content (Serves 4)

- 395 calories per serving
- 20 g protein
- Carbohydrates: 45 g

- 15 g fat

Ingredients

- 250g drained canned chickpeas
- 200g drained canned cannellini beans
- 200g tinned chopped tomatoes
- 2 tbsp olive oil
- 1 chopped red onion
- 190g sliced chorizo
- 3 red chopped chillis
- 1 tbsp paprika

Procedure

1. In a large skillet, heat 1 tablespoon olive oil over medium heat and cook the onion and chorizo for 5 minutes, or until lightly golden.

2. Whisk in the chickpeas and cannellini beans until thoroughly cooked.

3. Stir in the chopped tomatoes and paprika, then cover and cook for 5-10 minutes.

4. Serve with crusty brown bread, couscous, or brown rice for a hearty winter meal

MEDITERRANEAN SUPER SALAD

Quinoa's benefits cannot be overstated; this salad is high in protein and tasty to boot!

Nutrient Content

- 290 calories per serving
- 15 g protein
- Carbohydrates: 35 g

- 10 g fat

Ingredients

- 1 tsp olive oil
- 200g quinoa
- 12 red onion, finely chopped
- 2 tbsp mint, roughly chopped (fresh or dried)
- 400g Puy or Red lentils, rinsed and drained – you may buy dried lentils, but they must be soaked overnight.
- 14 cucumber (peeled and diced)
- 100g crumbled feta cheese
- 1 orange (zest and juice)
- 1 tablespoon red or white wine vinegar

Procedure

1. Cook the quinoa for 10-15 minutes in a large pot of boiling water until tender, then drain and set aside to cool.

2. In a medium-sized skillet, fry the onion in the oil.

3. Combine the quinoa, lentils, cucumber, feta, orange zest, chopped mint, and vinegar in a mixing bowl.

4. Serve chilled if possible!

5. Cooked chicken or lamb would be a delicious addition to this recipe for meat eaters!

ANABOLIC AVOCADO AND CHICKEN SALAD

A tasty and fresh salad that will satisfy meat eaters while holding you anabolic!

Nutrient Content

- 389 calories per serving
- 36 g protein
- Carbohydrates: 12 g
- 14g fat

Ingredients

- 12 peeled and sliced avocado
- 1 chopped beef tomato
- 14 sliced cucumber
- 2 tbsp olive oil
- 1 chicken breast
- Handful of watercress
- Handful of baby spinach
- Handful of rocket
- 12 peeled and sliced avocado
- 1 chopped beef tomato
- 14 sliced cucumber

Procedure

1. In a griddle pan, heat some olive oil over medium heat.

2. Cook the chicken breasts for 10 minutes on either side or until cooked through on the grill.

3. Toss the chicken breasts with the watercress, spinach, rocket, tomato, and sliced avocado and eat.

4. Drizzle olive oil over the salad to finish it off.

MUSCLE BUILDING STEAK & CHEESE SALAD

A good muscle-building salad that is simple and easy to prepare.

Nutrient Content (Serves 2)

- 308 calories per serving
- 34 g protein
- Carbohydrates: 15 g
- 14g fat

Ingredients

- 250 frying beef steak
- 1 chopped red onion
- 1 teaspoon crushed garlic
- Handful of baby spinach
- Handful of watercress
- Handful of lettuce
- 4 chopped baby tomatoes
- 2 tbsp balsamic vinegar
- 1 tbsp olive oil
- 50g blue cheese

Procedure

1. Season the steak with salt and pepper.

2. Heat a griddle pan over high heat with a tablespoon of olive oil.

3. Place the steak in the pan and cook for an additional 8 minutes, turning halfway through. Remove the steak from the pan and set it aside to cool.

4. Remove the steak from the pan and cut it into 2cm slices, then return it to the pan and cook for another minute over medium heat.

5. Combine the diced tomatoes, watercress, baby spinach, lettuce, garlic, and onions in a mixing bowl. In a mixing bowl, combine the steak strips, vinegar, and 1 tbsp olive oil. Combine all of the ingredients and grate the blue cheese on top.

THE SAILOR SALAD

Spinach was good enough for the popular muscle-building sailor cartoon back then, and it'll be good enough for you now; add a generous portion of the sailor's catch, and you'll be growing bigger than he ever was.

Nutrient Content (Serves 4)

- 220 calories per serving
- 20 g protein
- Carbohydrates: 12.5 g
- 10 g fat

Ingredients

- 170g lean grilled chopped turkey breast (or turkey deli meat already cooked)
- 1 tbsp real bacon bits (you can cut up bacon and grill it yourself or buy it pre-packaged)
- 2 diced hard-boiled eggs
- 100g baby potatoes
- 1 deseeded and sliced red, yellow, and green pepper
- 1 peeled and sliced avocado (do this at the end or it will turn brown)
- 1 tablespoon balsamic vinegar
- A pinch of salt and pepper

Procedure

1. Bring a medium pot of water to a boil over high heat, then add the halved new potatoes and cook for 15-20 minutes, or according to package directions.

2. In a serving dish, combine the meats (once grilled and chopped if you're doing it yourself) with the spinach and peppers.

3. Drain the potatoes and set aside to cool as you prepare the eggs in a small saucepan. Cook medium-boiled eggs for 8 minutes or hard-boiled eggs for 10 minutes.

4. Peel the eggs after running them under cold water. Dice and toss with your salad (this is where you can peel and add the avocado).

5. Season to taste with balsamic vinegar and salt and pepper.

HUNKED UP HALLOUMI

Since it's so chunky and filling, this cheese could almost pass for beef!

Nutrient Content (Serves 4)

- 461 calories per serving
- 29 g protein
- Carbohydrates: 3 g
- 37 g fat

Ingredients

- 2 tbsp white wine vinegar
- 2 tbsp olive oil
- 12 red onion thinly sliced
- Handful of rocket leaves

- 12 lemon juice
- Handful of green/black olives
- 500g sliced halloumi cheese
- 1 tbsp mayonnaise
- 12 chopped cucumber

Procedure

1. Prepare the grill by preheating it.

2. Drizzle 1 tsp olive oil on a baking tray and grill for 5 minutes, rotating once, until browned and crisp on the edges.

3. Toss the chopped olives, rocket, cucumber, and red onion with 1 tablespoon olive oil and a squeeze of lemon juice in a mixing bowl.

4. Add the mayonnaise and season with pepper (optional).

5. For an Aegean twist, serve alone or with crusty brown pita breads.

TUNA, SPINACH & QUINOA SALAD

For muscle building and fat loss, a quick and simple tuna salad is ideal.

Nutrient Content (Serves 2)

- 302 calories per serving
- 18 g protein
- Carbohydrates: 28 g
- 13 g fat

Ingredients

- 2 cans tuna in olive oil
- 1 chopped red onion

- 300g chopped peppers
- 1 tbsp olive oil
- 1 chopped red chilli
- 225g quinoa
- 350g halved cherry tomatoes
- 20g chopped black olives

Procedure

1. Cook the quinoa for 10–15 minutes until tender in a large pot of boiling water, then drain.

2. In a medium-sized skillet, heat the oil and cook the onions, peppers, and chili until softened.

3. In a mixing bowl, combine the drained quinoa, onion mixture, onions, salmon, baby spinach, and olives.

4. Finally, serve and enjoy.

STRENGTH CHICKEN AND SESAME SALAD

Three types of protein are included to meet all of your muscle-building requirements.

Nutrient Content (Serves 2)

- 430 calories per serving
- 20 g protein
- Carbohydrates: 16 g
- 15 g fat

Ingredients

- 2 chicken breasts
- 3 tbsp sesame oil
- 2 tsp grated ginger
- 1 crushed garlic clove
- 1 chopped red chilli
- 1 diced red onion
- Handful of basil leaves
- Handful of coriander leaves
- 100g baby spinach leaves
- 1 tsp sesame seeds
- 4 chopped almonds

Procedure

1. Prepare the grill by preheating it.

2. In a mixing bowl, combine 2 tablespoons sesame oil, chopped red chili, crushed garlic, and ginger. Combine all of the ingredients in a large mixing bowl.

3. Make a few deep cuts in the chicken breasts and marinate them for around 3 hours in the mixture.

4. In a mixing bowl, combine the spinach leaves, coriander leaves, basil leaves, red onion, sliced almonds, and sesame seeds.

5. Remove the chicken from the marinade and brush with the remaining marinade before grilling for 10 minutes on each side or until completely cooked.

6. Remove the chicken from the bone and place it in the salad bowl in strips.

7. Toss in the mandarin and drizzle 1 tbsp sesame oil over the salad before serving.

SIZZLING SALMON SALAD

Some people like it humid. You can make this dish with either warm or cold salmon; either way, it's filling and delicious.

Nutrient Content

- 521 calories per serving
- 46 g protein
- Carbohydrates: 24 g
- 27 g fat

Ingredients

- 150g salmon fillet
- 6 cherry tomatoes
- 100g couscous
- 3 asparagus stems (chop off the very end of the base but leave the rest intact)
- 50g diced low-fat mozzarella cheese
- 1 bell pepper sliced
- 1 tbsp balsamic vinegar
- 1 tbsp olive oil

Procedure

1. Prepare the grill by preheating it.

2. Pour boiling water over the couscous in the kettle (about 1cm over the top of the couscous, cover and leave to steam)

3. Cook salmon for 10-15 minutes on the grill, or until completely cooked. Set to the side.

4. Remove the cover from the couscous and stir with a fork to break up the grains.

5. Toss the couscous with the chili, mozzarella, and halved cherry tomatoes.

6. Grill the asparagus for 3-4 minutes, rotating every few minutes, until lightly browned on the surface.

7. Toss the asparagus with the salmon on a bed of couscous and drizzle with olive oil and balsamic vinegar until it's finished.

8. Season with salt and pepper to taste.

ROASTED BEETROOT, GOATS' CHEESE & EGG SALAD

If you like it or not, beetroot is a superfood that contains nutrients that are rarely found in your five daily servings! If you've never tried it before, or if you have, try this variation.

Nutrient Content

- 363 calories per serving
- 11 g protein
- Carbohydrates: 18 g
- 28g fat

Ingredients

- 200g cooked chopped beetroot (not in vinegar)
- 2 tbsp olive oil
- 1 orange's juice
- 2 eggs
- 1 tsp white wine vinegar
- 2 tbsp crème fraîche

- 1 tsp Dijon mustard
- A few stalks of dill, finely chopped (fresh or dried)
- 70g baby gem lettuce
- Handful of walnuts
- 100g crumbled goats cheese

Procedure

1. Preheat the oven to 200°C/400°F/Gas Mark 6 (200°C/400°F/Gas Mark 6).

2. Toss the beets with the orange juice in a lightly oiled baking tray and season with salt and pepper.

3. Roast for 20-25 minutes, rotating once during the baking process. Apply a little more olive oil if they start to dry out.

4. Meanwhile, bring a pot of water to a boil for the eggs. Reduce the heat to low and cook for 8 minutes (4 minutes if you prefer runny yolks), then run under cold water to cool. Peel and cut in half.

5. Toss together the remaining oil, crème fraîche, mustard, a teaspoon of white wine vinegar, and chopped dill. This is the salad dressing you'll use on your lettuce.

HERBY TUNA STEAK

Protein, protein, protein!

Nutrient Content (Serves 2)

- 578 calories per serving
- 35 g protein

- Carbohydrates: 3 g
- 48 g fat

Ingredients

- 2x 200g dolphin-friendly yellow fin tuna steaks
- 1 tbsp olive oil
- 2 lemon wedges
- 2 handfuls flat-leaf parsley and 2 handfuls coriander very roughly chopped
- 2 garlic cloves finely chopped
- 12 onion finely chopped
- Handful chopped green olives
- Half a lemon's juice

Procedure

1. Make the herby salad by combining the herbs with half of the chopped garlic, lemon juice, and olive oil.

2. Use a tea towel to crush the nuts or a blender to puree them. Add them to the herbs and mix well.

3. Drizzle olive oil over the tuna steaks and season with salt and pepper.

4. Preheat a dry pan to a very high temperature (look out for the smoke)

5. Cook the tuna for one minute on each side in the pan (if you have a griddle pan or grill then you should place these against the lines to get that nice straight off the BBQ look and taste)

6. Cook for 2 minutes on each side for medium, 3 minutes for medium well, and 4 minutes for well cooked if you like your tuna less pink (approximate times).

7. Once cooked, serve immediately with a herby salad (pour this over as a dressing or on the side as an accompaniment)

CHAPTER 9: DESSERTS

JASON'S PEANUT PROTEIN BARS

These tasty, homemade protein bars will help you save money!

Nutrient Content (Makes 12 bars)

- 386 calories per bar
- 18 g protein
- Carbohydrates: 24 g
- 6 g fat

Ingredients

- 4 scoops vanilla protein powder (optional)
- 400g rolled oats
- 340g almond butter
- 250ml coconut cream

Procedure

1. In a mixing bowl, whisk the coconut cream until smooth, then add the protein powder and almond butter and thoroughly combine.

2. Pour the oats into the mixing bowl and thoroughly combine.

3. Scoop the mixture into a baking tray and smooth it out until it's smooth.

4. Place the tray in the refrigerator for at least 8 hours.

5. Cut the dough into 12 bars.

COTTAGE CHEESECAKE

Enjoy this hearty, protein-rich cheesecake!

Nutrient Content

- 487 calories per serving
- 43 g protein
- Carbohydrates: 53 g
- 7g fat

Ingredients

- 1 scoop vanilla protein powder
- 150g fat-free cottage cheese
- 1 tbsp sugar-free instant pudding mix
- 5 tbsp low-fat milk
- 1 package stevia
- Strawberries, a few

Procedure

1. In a blender, combine all of the ingredients and blend until smooth.

2. Arrange in a bowl with the strawberries on top.

POWER PARFAIT

A delectable dessert that looks as good as it tastes. It has a whopping 38 grams of protein in it.

Nutrient Content

- 254 calories per serving
- 38 g protein
- Carbohydrates: 21 g
- 2 g fat

Ingredients

- 1 scoop protein powder (vanilla)
- 200ml Greek yogurt
- 50g mixed berries

Procedure

1. Combine the yogurt and protein powder in a mixing bowl.

2. Fill a tall parfait glass halfway with berries and yogurt and set aside.

BANANA PROTEIN PUDDING

This is something I would recommend all of the time, but if you want to treat yourself, this is a fast and easy pudding that tastes great and has a good amount of protein.

Nutrient Content (Serves 4)

- 357 calories per serving
- 30 g protein
- Carbohydrates: 22 g
- 20 g fat

Ingredients

- 4 scoops vanilla protein powder
- 100 grams low-fat butter
- 2 bananas, chopped
- 100 g self-raising flour
- 2 tsp ground cinnamon
- 2 eggs
- 2 tbsp low-fat milk

Procedure

1. Place the butter in a serving bowl. Microwave for 30 seconds, or until fully melted. In a mixing bowl, mash 1 banana. After that, combine the protein powder, rice, cinnamon, eggs, and milk.

2. Sprinkle the remaining chopped banana on top of the mixture. Cook for 8-9 minutes in the microwave, or until the pudding has risen and is thoroughly cooked through.

GREEK YOGURT WITH HONEY AND BERRIES

A fast and simple dessert with a whopping 43 grams of protein.

Nutrient Content

- 522 calories per serving
- 43 g protein
- Carbohydrates: 86 g
- 7g fat

Ingredients

- 1 scoop vanilla protein powder (optional)
- 45g berries
- 100g Greek yogurt
- 4 tbsp honey

Procedure

1. Combine all of your ingredients and you'll have a light and nutritious dessert with no guilt. For added crunch, sprinkling flaked almonds on top is a good idea.

CHAPTER 10: SIDES

LEMON AND MOROCCAN MINT COUSCOUS

A tangy, fresh side dish that pairs well with fish, chicken, vegetables, and even lamb and beef.

Nutrient Content (Serves 2)

- 367 calories per serving
- 6 g protein
- Carbohydrates: 43 g
- 20 g fat

Ingredients

- 250g couscous
- 2 tablespoons lemon zest and juice
- 20g new mint
- 4 tablespoons toasted pine nuts

Procedure

1. Pour boiling water over the dried couscous in a serving bowl (it should cover the couscous by about a cm on top) and cover with a plate to steam. If desired, season with a chicken/vegetable stock cube added to the boiling water.

2. After a few minutes of steaming, expose the couscous and fluff up the grains with a fork.

3. Combine the lemon zest and juice, finely chopped mint, and pine nuts in a large mixing bowl.

4. Season to taste and drizzle with olive oil before serving.

SWEET POTATO WEDGES

You won't be the only one who enjoys these delectable wedges.

Nutrient Content

- 207 calories per serving
- 3 g protein
- Carbohydrates: 38 g
- 6 g fat

Ingredients

- 4 sweet potatoes, scrubbed and cut into big wedges
- 2 tablespoons extra virgin olive oil
- 3-4 garlic cloves
- A sprig or two of rosemary

Procedure

1. Preheat oven to 350°F/180°C/Gas Mark 4 (350°F/180°C/Gas Mark 4).

2. Toss the wedges in olive oil after you've scrubbed the skin of the sweet potatoes (don't strip it) with a kitchen scourer or something rough enough.

3. Arrange the wedges on a baking tray, scattering rosemary sprigs on top and inserting whole garlic cloves in their skin over and around them. Preheat the oven to 350°F and bake the whole thing for 30-40 minutes, or until crispy.

MUSHROOM RISOTTO

Another side dish that goes well with chicken breast. It's perfect for a post-workout snack!

Nutrient Content (Serves 2)

- 445 calories per serving
- 15 g protein
- Carbohydrates: 63 g
- 17g fat

Ingredients

- 50g dried porcini mushrooms
- 250g sliced and washed pack chestnut mushrooms
- 2 tablespoons olive oil
- 1 finely chopped onion
- 2 finely chopped garlic cloves
- 300g Arborio rice
- 175 milliliters of white wine
- 50g freshly grated parmesan or grana padano
- A handful of chopped tarragon leaves

Procedure

1. Soak the dried porcini mushrooms in 1 litre boiling water for 20 minutes before draining into a separate tub (keep the liquid at this point as you need to add to the risotto later).

2. Slice the mushrooms thinly.

3. In a large frying pan, heat the oil over medium heat and fry the onions and garlic for around 5 minutes, or until tender.

4. Add the dried and fresh chestnut mushrooms at this stage and stir for another 5 minutes, or until softened.

5. Whisk in the rice for about a minute before pouring in the wine.

6. Bring to a low simmer (bubbling), then add a quarter of the mushroom stock.

8. Continue adding the stock a quarter at a time, waiting for the rice to absorb the liquid between additions.

9. Once the rice is soft, a lot of stirring is needed! Continue to add small quantities of water if the liquid runs out and the rice is still a little rough.

10. Remove the pan from the heat and stir in half of the cheese and the tarragon leaves. Allow the pan to steam for a few minutes after covering it.

11. Garnish with the remaining cheese and herbs!

HOT & SPICY BUTTERNUT SQUASH

Squash is a winner that is always overlooked in our fruit and vegetable collection. One squash can feed a family, and if you're dining alone, you can freeze it and use it later!

Nutrient Content (Serves 4)

- 227 calories per serving
- 1 gram of protein
- Carbohydrates: 30 g
- 14g fat

Ingredients

- 1 butternut squash
- 4 tablespoons olive oil
- 4 tablespoons honey
- 1 deseeded and finely chopped red scotch bonnet chili

Procedure

1. Preheat the oven to 200°C/400°F/gas 6 (200°C/400°F/gas 6).

2. Remove the top and bottom of the butternut squash and chop them. After that, you could break it in half lengthwise. You should be able to strip the skin with a vegetable peeler now, but if that doesn't work, take a sharp knife and cut downwards.

3. Now, hollow out the seeds from the base with a spoon.

4. Now you can slice horizontally into thick (1-2 cm) slices.

5. Arrange the slices in a single layer on a lightly oiled baking tray.

6. Drizzle the honey liberally over the slices and liberally sprinkle the chopped chili (or to your heat tolerance!)

7. Bake for 35-40 minutes, or until golden brown and crispy.

8. Some leftovers can be frozen in a sealable sandwich bag and reheated in the oven until ready to eat.

MUSTARDY CAULIFLOWER CHEESE

A Winter Warmer that can be eaten alone or as a side dish.

Nutrient Content (Serves 2)

- 240 calories per serving
- 15 g protein
- Carbohydrates: 14 g
- 12 g fat

Ingredients

- 1 whole cauliflower
- 2 tablespoons wholegrain mustard
- 100g low-fat cheddar cheese
- 100ml low-fat crème fraiche

Procedure

1. Chop the cauliflower by removing the thickest portion of the stem and pushing the florets apart.

2. Toss the cauliflower, 34% of the cheese, crème fraîche, and mustard in a mixing bowl.

3. Place in an oven dish and bake for 30 minutes at 200°C/400°F/gas 6 in a preheated oven.

4. Sprinkle the remaining cheese over the top of the dish and grill for 5-7 minutes, or until the cheese is browned and bubbling.

FRUITY NUTTY QUINOA

Are you stumped as to what to do with your quinoa? This recipe is perfectly delicious and goes well with almost every main course.

Nutrient Content (Serves 4)

- 328 calories per serving
- 10 g protein
- Carbohydrates: 36 g
- 15 g fat

Ingredients

- 200g quinoa
- 6 dried apricots
- 1 lemon's juice
- 2 tbsp olive oil
- A pinch of salt and pepper
- A handful of chopped parsley and mint

- 50g cashew nuts

Procedure

1. Cook the quinoa in a large pot of boiling water for 10–15 minutes, or until tender, then drain.

2. In a mixing bowl, combine the quinoa, apricots, spices, lemon juice, zest, and olive oil, as well as some salt and pepper.

3. Sprinkle the cashews on top and serve.

RICE & PEAS

With this simple side dish, you can transport yourself to the Caribbean.

Nutrient Content (Serves 2)

- 430 calories per serving
- 20 g protein
- Carbohydrates: 16 g
- 15 g fat

Ingredients

- 300g brown rice
- 75ml olive oil
- 200g dried kidney beans
- 1 teaspoon chili powder

Procedure

1. Soak the kidney beans overnight in water (you can buy canned kidney beans and use them right away if you're in a hurry, but you won't get the same authentic color or flavor!)

2. In a large saucepan over high heat, bring the liquid and kidney beans to a boil (add water if you need to).

3. Add the rice and cook for 30 minutes, draining halfway through. Keep the rice in the pan, add the kidney beans, and cook for 4 minutes covered.

4. Toss your rice with a pinch of chili powder and eat.

MUSCLE RICE SALAD

This tasty and nutritious side dish will spice up your regular brown rice.

Nutrient Content (Serves 2)

- 454 calories per serving
- 11 g protein
- Carbohydrates: 64 g
- 19g fat

Ingredients

- 1 deseeded and finely chopped red pepper
- 12 cucumber finely chopped
- 1 big grated carrot
- 10 chopped cherry tomatoes
- 2 tablespoons olive oil

Procedure

1. Fill a pot halfway with cold water and heat on high until the water boils.

2. When the water is boiling, add the rice and cook for 20 minutes. After that, drain.

3. Combine the rice, diced red pepper, cucumber, grated carrot, and cherry tomatoes in a mixing bowl and drizzle with olive oil.

CHAPTER 11: HOMEMADE PROTEIN SHAKES

CHOCO COFFEE ENERGY SHAKE

Replace your morning caffeine fix with this energizing alternative.

Nutrient Content

- 299 calories per serving
- 42 g protein

- Carbohydrates: 14 g
- 6 g fat

Ingredients

- 2 scoops chocolate protein powder (optional)
- 100 mL low-fat milk
- 1 cup water
- 1 tablespoon instant coffee

Procedure

1. In a blender, combine all of the ingredients and blend until smooth.

2. Have fun.

PEACHY PUNCH

This peachy punch will please your sweet tooth while still giving you 50 grams of protein.

Nutrient Content

- 543 calories per serving
- 50 g protein
- Carbohydrates: 57 g
- 11g fat
- 2 scoop vanilla protein powder (optional)

Ingredients

- 50g low-fat Greek yogurt
- 200ml low-fat milk
- 45g rolled oats

- 1 chopped peach
- 1 cup water

Procedure

1. In a blender, combine all of the ingredients and blend until smooth.

2. Have fun.

JASON'S HOMEMADE MASS GAINER

It can be difficult to obtain all of the calories required for growth. The majority of weight-gainers are high in empty calories which can be costly. This monster of a shake has about 1000 calories in it and 75 grams of protein to keep you growing.

Nutrient Content

- 970 calories per serving
- 75 g protein
- Carbohydrates: 90 g
- 30 g fat

Ingredients

- 2 scoop whey protein powder (chocolate)
- 2 cups whole milk
- 12 cup dry rolled oats
- 1 banana
- 2 tablespoons organic almond butter
- 1 cup broken ice

Procedure

1. In a blender, combine all of the ingredients and blend until smooth.

2. Have fun.

BLACKBERRY BRAWN

It's a quick and simple shake that's both tasty and nutritious.

Nutrient Content

- 457 calories per serving
- 47 g protein
- Carbohydrates: 30 g
- 16g fat

Ingredients

- 1 cup blackberries
- 200ml low-fat milk
- 2 tbsp flax seed oil
- 50g low-fat Greek yogurt
- 1 cup ice
- 2 scoops vanilla protein powder

Procedure

1. In a blender, combine all of the ingredients and blend until smooth.

2. Have fun.

LEAN AND MEAN PINEAPPLE SHAKE

This shake is new, tropical, and zingy, and it's packed with enough energy to keep you going until lunchtime!

Nutrient Content

- 355 calories per serving
- 23 g protein
- Carbohydrates: 65 g
- 3 g fat

Ingredients

- 1 banana
- 4 strawberries
- 1 cup chopped pineapple
- 1 tablespoon Greek yogurt (low-fat)
- 1 cup of water
- 1 scoop of vanilla protein powder

Procedure

1. In a blender, combine all of the ingredients and blend until smooth.

2. Have fun.

NO WHEY!

Is there no protein powder? This delicious, nutritious shake has enough protein to keep you rising!

Nutrient Content

- 388 calories per serving
- 26 g protein
- Carbohydrates: 32 g

- 22g fat

Ingredients

- 1 cup blackberries
- 1 cup strawberries
- 200ml low-fat milk
- 130g Greek yogurt
- 1 cup ice
- 1 tablespoon almond butter

Procedure

1. In a blender, combine all of the ingredients and blend until smooth.

2. Have fun.

CHOCOLATE PEANUT DELIGHT

This delicious shake will satisfy your chocolate cravings.

Nutrient Content

- 656 calories per serving
- 63 g protein
- Carbohydrates: 55 g
- 21g fat

Ingredients

- 1 scoop chocolate whey protein powder (optional)
- 1 cup Greek yogurt (low-fat)
- 1 banana, whole
- Peanut butter, 2 tbsp

- 1 ice cube

Procedure

1. In a blender, combine all of the ingredients and blend until smooth.

2. Have fun.

CARIBBEAN CRUSH

Exceptionally tasty!

Nutrient Content

- 263 calories per serving
- 25 g protein
- Carbohydrates: 38 g
- 3 g fat

Ingredients

- 1 scoop protein powder (of your choice)
- 12 chopped mango
- 12 cup pineapple chunks
- 1 peeled and cubed kiwi
- 1 strawberry
- 1 cup ice

Procedure

1. In a blender, combine all of the ingredients and blend until smooth.

2. Have fun.

CHOPPED ALMOND SMOOTHIE

This fast and easy shake will satisfy your chocolate craving while also providing 24 grams of protein.

Nutrient Content

- 241 calories per serving
- 24 g protein
- Carbohydrates: 6 g
- 13 g fat

Ingredients

- 1 scoop chocolate protein powder
- 12 cup water
- 17 diced almonds
- 12 teaspoon coconut extract

Procedure

1. In a blender, combine all of the ingredients and blend until smooth.

2. Have fun.

CHOCOLATE & RASPBERRY BANG

A delicious and fast protein shake that will keep you growing and shredding!

Nutrient Content

- 269 calories per serving

- 31 g protein
- Carbohydrates: 16 g
- 9 g fat

Ingredients

- 2 scoops chocolate protein powder (optional)
- 12 cup raspberries
- 200 milliliters whole milk
- 12 cup ice cubes

Procedure

1. In a blender, combine all of the ingredients and blend until smooth.

2. Have fun.

BERRY PROTEIN SHAKE

It's perfect for a hot summer day and can be used at any time of year.

Nutrient Content

- 342 calories per serving
- 38 g protein
- Carbohydrates: 42 g
- 3 g fat

Ingredients

- Whey protein powder (two scoops)
- 1 cup blueberries
- 1 cup blackberries

- 1 cup raspberry berries
- 1 cup water
- 1 cup ice

Procedure

1. In a blender, combine all of the ingredients and blend until smooth.

2. Have fun.

CINNAMON SURPRISE

To please your taste buds, make a quick and easy protein shake!

Nutrient Content

- 244 calories per serving
- 47 g protein
- Carbohydrates: 7 g
- 4 g fat

Ingredients

- 2 scoops chocolate protein powder (optional)
- 1 tablespoon cinnamon
- 1 cup water
- 1 cup ice

Procedure

1. In a blender, combine all of the ingredients and blend until smooth.

2. Have fun.

VANILLA STRAWBERRY SURPRISE

Nothing will take you back to a day at the beach like this – it tastes incredible and is deceptively good at filling you up while still helping you bulk up and shed weight.

Nutrient Content

- 329 calories per serving
- 36 g protein
- Carbohydrates: 42 g
- 2 g fat

Ingredients

- 2 scoops vanilla protein powder (optional)
- 1 banana
- 4 new or frozen strawberries
- 1 cup of ice

Procedure

1. In a blender, combine all of the ingredients and blend until smooth.

2. Have fun.

PUMPKIN POWER

This shake has a fantastic flavor and is high in protein.

Nutrient Content

- 224 calories per serving
- 38 g protein

- Carbohydrates: 14 g
- 3 g fat

Ingredients

- 2 scoops vanilla protein powder (optional)
- 1 cup pumpkin, diced
- 1 tsp cinnamon
- 1 cup water

Procedure

1. In a blender, combine all of the ingredients and blend until smooth.

2. Have fun.

FRESH STRAWBERRY SHAKE

All year long, keep it easy with this strawberry shake.

Nutrient Content

- 303 calories per serving
- 35 g protein
- Carbohydrates: 15 g
- 11g fat

Ingredients

- 2 scoops vanilla protein powder (optional)
- 1 cup strawberries

- 2 cups water
- 1 tablespoon flaxseed oil

Procedure

1. In a blender, combine all of the ingredients and blend until smooth.

2. Have fun.

BREAKFAST BANANA SHAKE

You don't have much time? This breakfast shake has a lot of flavor and will give you a good start to your day.

Nutrient Content

- 566 calories per serving
- 59 g protein
- Carbohydrates: 69g
- 6 g fat

Ingredients

- 1 banana
- 200ml low-fat milk
- 2 scoops vanilla whey protein powder
- 100g rolled oats

Procedure

1. In a blender, combine all of the ingredients and blend until smooth.

2. Have fun.

Conversion Tables

VOLUME EQUIVALENTS (LIQUID)

US STANDARD	US STANDARD (OUNCES)	METRIC
2 tablespoons	1 fl. oz.	30 mL
¼ cup	2 fl. oz.	60 mL
½ cup	4 fl. oz.	120 mL
1 cup	8 fl. oz.	240mL
1½ cups	12 fl. oz.	355 mL
2 cups or 1 pint	16 fl. oz.	475 mL
4 cups or 1 quart	32 fl. oz.	1 L
1 gallon	128 fl. oz.	4 L

OVEN TEMPERATURES

FAHRENHEIT (°F)	CELSIUS (°C) APPROXIMATE
250 °F	120 °C
300 °F	150 °C
325 °F	165 °C
350 °F	180 °C
375 °F	190 °C
400 °F	200 °C
425 °F	220 °C
450 °F	230 °C

VOLUME EQUIVALENTS (LIQUID)

US STANDARD	METRIC (APPROXIMATE)
⅛ teaspoon	0.5 mL
¼ teaspoon	1 mL
½ teaspoon	2 mL
⅔ teaspoon	4 mL
1 teaspoon	5 mL
1 tablespoon	15 mL
¼ cup	59 mL
⅓ cup	79 mL
½ cup	118 mL
⅔ cup	156 mL
¾ cup	177 mL
1 cup	235 mL
2 cups or 1 pint	475 mL
3 cups	700 mL
4 cups or 1 quart	1 L
½ gallon	2 L
1 gallon	4 L

WEIGHT EQUIVALENTS

US STANDARD	METRIC (APPROXIMATE)
½ ounce	15 g
1 ounce	30 g
2 ounces	60 g
4 ounces	115 g
8 ounces	225 g
12 ounces	340 g
16 ounces or 1 pound	455 g

CONCLUSION

Thank you for reading this book and having the patience to try the recipes.

I do hope that you have had as much enjoyment reading and experimenting with the meals as I have had writing the book.

If you would like to leave a comment, you can do so at the Order section->Digital orders, in your Amazon account.

Stay safe and healthy!

Made in United States
North Haven, CT
17 April 2023

35566241R00075